PENGUIN BOOKS

WHERE WERE YOU?

Matthew Friedman is a leading, internationally renowned global expert on modern slavery and human trafficking with over thirty-five years of experience as a manager, programme designer, evaluator, and front-line responder. An award-winning public speaker, author, filmmaker, and philanthropist, Matthew regularly advises heads of governments and intelligence agencies.

As the Founder and CEO of the Mekong Club, a consortium of global business leaders who are pledged to help fight human trafficking, Matthew is considered the leading catalyst of the anti-slavery movement in Asia's business sector by captains of industry.

In 2017, Matthew received the prestigious 'Asia Communicator of the Year Gold Award' for giving more than 800 presentations to 80,000 people, including government leaders and the Vatican, on the topic of modern slavery within a five-year period in multiple countries. Matthew has a unique and powerful speaking style that inspires people and helps them reach their fullest potential.

Each year, he is cited at least forty times in news media, such as CNN, Bloomberg, Reuters, Associated Press, the *Financial Times*, and *The Economist*, and he is invited to speak at major international conferences around the world.

He has managed and directed tens of millions of dollars to major humanitarian portfolios for the World Bank, the US State Department, and the United Nations, impacting millions of lives. His work over the last thirty-five years, pioneering and managing international anti-human trafficking projects in Nepal, Bangladesh, Thailand, and Hong Kong, has given him access to many influential networks in different countries throughout the world.

Matthew is the author of thirteen books ranging from action novels, non-fiction accounts of his anti-human trafficking work, to a book that outlines his unique philosophy of 'time'. A long-time supporter of film and the media arts, Matthew was an executive producer and advisor on four award-winning films, one of which was nominated for an Emmy and another of which was executive-produced by Emma Thompson.

Matthew provides a range of inspirational keynote speeches to teach, mentor and motivate people from all walks of life to step up and take a stand in life. He has an uncanny ability to take something as complicated and confusing as slavery and break it down into a series of simple messages that walk a person down a path to understanding. He has shifted the mindsets of many—even the most resistant detractors. His is always a message of hope.

Matthew is married to Sylvia Yu Friedman who is an award-winning journalist, filmmaker, international speaker, and author of *Silenced No More: Voices of Comfort Women* who also fights the scourge of modern slavery. Together, in the summer of 2016, they gave 113 presentations in twenty-seven US cities.

ADVANCE PRAISE FOR *WHERE WERE YOU?*

'Matt's grasp of the issue(s) of human trafficking is thirty years deep, and reflects a long journey of action and reflection which he graciously allows us to learn from. There is something here for all of us, and indeed it will TAKE all of us to end human trafficking. That's the moral of Matt's superb book.'

-Jennifer Roemhildt Tunehag Co-founder, European Freedom Network Core team, Freedom Business Alliance Member, World Evangelical Alliance Global Human Trafficking Task Force

'Must read for all. I highly commend this book for everyone to read whether you are an inquirer or a veteran abolitionist. If you are a government employee, business person or NGO worker, this is a must read. There is a growing list of literature to read on the topic of slavery and human trafficking, this one should be one of the first to read. In this new and very readable profile of modern slavery, Matt Friedman gives a well-balanced take on the issue, his experience, and what each of us can do practically to join the "second generation abolition movement".'

-Peter J Mihaere, CEO, Stand Against Slavery

'*Where Were You?: A Profile of Modern Slavery* by Matthew S. Friedman, is a short text that has appeal for both the beginner and the veteran abolitionist. The theme of the book is really that of Friedman's personal experience as a counter trafficking agent over the past few decades... Overall, I really enjoyed reading this book. I felt the author's transparency was very inspiring.'

-Rachael Williams-Mejri, Editor, *Grace As Justice Magazine*

'Accounts Mr Friedman relates are disturbing, troubling, and overwhelming, but must be told. In often what seems too-vivid detail, he describes lives of some of the most forgotten and used unfortunates, who are mostly women.

Where Were You?, a readable, concise account of human suffering, must be read by all the fortunate enjoying a safe, comfortable life, to be enlightened that not all humans are so lucky. We Americans too easily dismiss human trafficking as something that happens "over there". Detailing the extent of the problem in the US, he honestly labels it what it is—slavery. Read it. You will be moved, angry, overwhelmed.'

-Frank Hilo

'Although often difficult to read due to its subject matter, members of the counter-trafficking community will find a wealth of valuable insights in this book about not only the world of slavery, but how to fight it.'

-B M Vance

'It is with great pleasure that I write in recommendation of Matthew S. Friedman.

Throughout the world there are many deeply committed individuals and organizations engaging in vital anti-slavery work. Matthew stands out among them for his pioneering and leadership work in the fight against human trafficking and modern slavery for more than thirty-five years. He has helped mobilize a small army of people around the world who have stepped up to be a part of an abolitionist movement.

Matthew currently is the CEO of the Mekong Club, an Asia-based global non-profit organization that enlists the support of the private sector to be active responders in the fight against modern slavery. He has recruited over a hundred business professionals and captains of industry to step up and use their expertise to participate in working groups, develop tools and promote pro-business agenda related to the anti-modern slavery movement. I believe The Mekong Club is a leader—uniting and mobilizing the private sector for a common cause—to disrupt and abolish modern slavery.

Since 1985, Matthew has worked for the US Government, United Nations, NGO and private sector, and his list of extraordinary milestones include:

- Giving presentations on human trafficking and modern slavery to over 120,000 people in thirty countries;
- He has completed speaking tours across five Asia Pacific Countries: Singapore, Japan, Sri Lanka, Australia, and Bangladesh;

- Matthew and his two adult sons completed an eighteen-day road trip across the USA to reach companies, schools, and the general public to promote an abolitionist campaign (over 10,000 people reached through twenty-five events);
- With his wife Sylvia, they have completed a seventy road-trip speaking tour across the USA (114 presentations to over 15,000 people reached);
- Raised over US$18 million for a range of programs implemented by the UN, US government and NGOs;
- Helped to set up national anti-trafficking programs in nine countries to best utilize their available resources to have the most impact;
- Managed two major regional government platforms to bring about multi-lateral collaboration between countries;
- Provided technical assistance to twenty-three governments to help them refine and improve their anti-human trafficking program efforts;
- Advised fourteen global donors to help them make more responsible funding decisions;
- Developed eleven country/regional training programs to train UN, NGO and legal responders;
- Provided funding to over thirty-five NGOs, helping to directly rescue 2,000 victims;
- Media interviews on human trafficking and modern slavery with over 300 American and international TV, radio, and press articles and stories;
- Set up one of the first business to business organizations working with the private sector—the Mekong Club non-profit which has helped rescue more than 2,200 people in slavery;
- Published three books on modern slavery out of his twelve books (including a Penguin Random House book to be published this November 2021);
- Helped in the production of three award-winning films including one Emmy award-nominated;
- Catalyzed and supported a range of cutting-edge research to help understand the issue to help establish better responses;
- Interviewed and directly worked with over 2,000 trafficked persons; and
- Funded the MTV Exit media platform during his time at USAID—reaching millions with prevention messages.

Matthew's most important milestone was his book project that involved interviewing over 350 young girls who had been trafficked from Nepal to

India. Five years later, nearly all of them had died of HIV/AIDS. Their premature deaths had a profound impact on Matthew and motivated him to commit his entire life to the fight against this global scourge. He inspires us greatly to believe that we can make a difference and help end this evil and ancient form of human slavery in our generation.

I commend Matthew Friedman for his outstanding work as a pioneer in the field of fighting modern slavery.'

- U.S. Senator Max Cleland (Ret.)

Where Were You?
A Profile of
Modern Slavery

Matthew S. Friedman

PENGUIN BOOKS
An imprint of Penguin Random House

PENGUIN BOOKS

USA | Canada | UK | Ireland | Australia
New Zealand | India | South Africa | China | Southeast Asia

Penguin Books is part of the Penguin Random House group of companies
whose addresses can be found at global.penguinrandomhouse.com

Published by Penguin Random House SEA Pte Ltd
9, Changi South Street 3, Level 08-01,
Singapore 486361

First published in Penguin Books by Penguin Random House SEA 2021

ISBN 9789814954433

www.penguin.sg

Table of Contents

Dedication

This book is dedicated to my wife, Sylvia, who helped me find myself and come to understand the true meaning of love. To my two sons, Brandon and Damien—your transition into fine young men continues to provide a constant source of pride and joy. To my father, who has always been my intellectual inspiration—I thank you for your unconditional love and acceptance. You will always remain the source of light that reveals the infinite knowledge and wisdom that this world has to offer. To my mother, I thank you for the compassion and empathy you instilled in me, which helped me listen to and hear the voices of need among those who have suffered. To all of my mentors, friends, and family, I thank you for helping me get to where I am today. Without you, this book would not have been possible.

Finally, I'd like to dedicate this book to the many victims of modern slavery. It is my hope and dream that we, the world, will someday find a way to end modern slavery in our time.

Foreword

The book you are about to read is not an ordinary book. Neither is it a pleasant nor a nice book. The book you are about to read is an urgent book. It is urgent because it will give you an unusual insight into one of the world's most compelling tragedies—that of modern-day slavery. It is urgent because, in our world anno 2020, there are over 40 million modern slaves. It is urgent because this number is higher than ever before in the history of humankind.

Slaves are not only victims of human trafficking; slaves are all those who, against their will, work in the sex industry; who get no pay or are not decently paid in construction work; who are abused in the fishing industry, in the garment industry, the entertainment industry, and in so many other places. Therefore, we cannot say that this is something that happened long ago or farther away. It happens now, and it happens here. Even worse, in our modern world, with so many people moving every day— voluntarily as migrants or forced as refugees—tens of thousands enter situations that make them vulnerable to becoming victims of modern slavery, human trafficking, sexual violence, and abuse.

We all have to face this truth: modern slavery is part of our lives. We cannot ignore it. Therefore, this book is urgent. It gives you an unusual insight into a complex matter. It will help you face the truth because it is full of practical insights and valuable tips. These facts are the result of Matthew Friedman's in-depth, first-hand knowledge by boots-on-the-ground work throughout dozens of Asian countries for over thirty years. But it is not only this knowledge. Most of all, I dare say, it is the way in which Matthew Friedman shares his knowledge. In this book, he tells us the stories of both victims and perpetrators of modern slavery and human trafficking, and by doing so he gives them a face and a voice.

'Where were you?' is a question that was once voiced by a victim of human trafficking. You will read her shocking story in this book. Now, through this urgent book, the question is passed on to you and to me, to all of us. I have no doubt that this question will grab you and will not let you go. It is my deep hope that this book will inspire many readers to become present-day abolitionists.

Kathleen Ferrier
Former Member of Parliament in the Netherlands

Part I

Meeting Suffering Slaves
on the Frontlines

Chapter 1

Discovering Sexual Slavery

May 1991. My assignment in Kathmandu, Nepal, seemed like a valuable two-year opportunity for a thirty year-old man. I had completed many short overseas assignments before this one, and I arrived with enthusiasm for my duties, but no particular expectations about this ancient country. I was assigned as a public health officer working for the United States Agency for International Development (USAID). Part of my job involved creating a range of programmes that would help improve the overall health status of the Nepalese people on a national scale. We'd identify an important health issue, work with the government and non-governmental organizations (NGOs) to construct a response, and then put this initiative into place. I usually took part in every step of the process, including data collection, programme design, implementation, and evaluation. It became a great learning experience for me that set the foundation for my entire career.

We discovered something very unusual: a significant number of teenage girls between the ages of thirteen and fifteen had contracted HIV/AIDS. In a traditional Hindu society like theirs, we couldn't understand how these girls had got this terrible disease. At first, we thought they had received blood transfusions tainted with HIV. There was no explanation that made sense to us.

The truth of the matter

To understand the problem, we visited a number of shelters where these girls lived. What we learned completely shocked us. The girls repeatedly told the same story: someone had tricked them into leaving their community, only to face a life of sexual slavery in neighbouring India. It wasn't just one or two stories like this—there were literally hundreds.

A typical story went like this: a trafficker, often a young, handsome man in his mid-twenties, would enter a village and begin flashing money around to show that he was rich. While hanging out at tea stalls, he'd talk about how he wanted to find a rural wife. He would state that he didn't want an urban wife; they were 'too much trouble.' After locating a young girl he found attractive, he would befriend her and eventually ask for her hand in marriage. Seeing this as an opportunity to benefit their daughter and the entire family, the parents often agreed without hesitation. The wedding would take place immediately, with the entire village in attendance.

After the wedding, the trafficker would tell the family he was taking their daughter to the capital, Kathmandu, to live. He would say he'd return in three or four months for another visit. But instead, he'd take her to Mumbai, India. The uneducated teenage 'bride' who had never travelled for more than twenty kilometres from home wouldn't even realize they had left Nepal.

Upon arriving in Mumbai, the man would immediately take his bride to the red-light district. Once there, he'd put her in a small room and say he'd return shortly. By this point, the girl would begin to wonder what was happening. Seeing all of these young girls dressed in revealing clothes wouldn't make any sense to her. But, accepting her husband's word, she'd do as she was told.

The man would then go off to meet the 'madam' and collect $600 from the sale of his wife to the brothel. Depending on her age and attractiveness, this number could be higher or lower. The money stood as profit on top of the gold he acquired from the wedding ceremony. He'd also hand over a few wedding photos. Upon completing this transaction, he'd return to Nepal to carry out this same scam again and again. Some traffickers sold over sixty young girls a year.

The madam would then enter the room and tell the girl that her husband had just sold her to the brothel and that she would now have to have sex with many men every day. The girl's initial reaction would invariably be utter disbelief. 'My husband wouldn't do this to me! He loves me! This is a mistake!' The madam's stern response would quickly bring this attitude into check.

After the young girl finally comprehended her fate, she would declare she'd rather kill herself before doing those shameful things. In response to this expected tactic, the madam would pull out the wedding photos and start pointing at the girl's family members: 'Is this your mother, your father, your brother? If you hurt yourself, we will hurt them. Do you understand me?' At this point, the girl would begin to truly fathom that she had been trapped in a living hell with no hope of escape.

To transform her into a prostitute, the process was very simple. All they needed to do was to shame her. This was done by bringing five or six professional rapists together to 'break her in.' During this process, they'd beat her, swear at her, rape her, and do everything they could to humiliate her. The more she resisted, the more they would push back. Within forty-eight hours, she might be raped up to thirty times. The objective of this process was to completely destroy her will so that she would lay back and accept whomever they brought to her. Nearly all the girls I interviewed suffered a variation of this horrific 'training and breaking' process. Over the years, the brothels had honed this procedure down to surgical precision. There was no alternative other than complete submission.

Once the girl had been broken, she'd be forced to have sex every day with up to ten men. She would receive no respite, even during her menstrual period or if she grew ill. To get through the days, many girls would turn to drugs or alcohol to dull the edge of their misery. Since they couldn't make customers use condoms, most would acquire a vast array of sexually transmitted diseases, including HIV/AIDS.

I remember one girl telling me how hard it was to cope with this daily hell: 'Three o'clock in the morning was the hardest time for me. I would have been with at least eight or nine men by this time. Sometimes more. I would be expected to see one or two more. I used to be so tired. My body smelled of sweat and semen. All I wanted was to climb into bed and die. My life was a nightmare that simply wouldn't go away.'

To maintain order and ensure the madam's absolute authority, the brothel community had a small army of thugs called *goondas*. They ensured that the girls did whatever they were told. If a girl showed any sign of resistance, she would be severely beaten or even tortured with cigarettes, electric shocks, or by having a knife placed up against her throat. Common scare tactics included exposing the girls to snakes and cockroaches. The more a girl resisted, the more she would be punished.

In addition to providing security within the brothels, musclemen regularly patrolled the narrow lanes, bus depots, and train stations, searching for runaway girls like packs of wild dogs in search of prey. With this kind of surveillance, those on the run had little hope of escape. If one managed to get away, it was usually not long before a *goonda* squad picked her up and returned her to the brothel for punishment. Now and then, an escapee would be brutally murdered to send a message to the others: 'If you go against us, this will happen to you.' The madams often showed photographs of these murders to get the point across to new victims. Following a raid in a brothel, it was not uncommon to find a madam's phone filled with graphic photos that could turn even the most hardened person's stomach.

After two or three years of unimaginable abuse, many of the girls would be so used up that they'd eventually stop attracting customers. One survivor described it like this: 'The girls who had been there for a long time began to get what we called "black eyes". It is this vacant stare that seemed as if she was not even alive any more. Her soul had already taken flight. Her body just went through the motions.'

To make room for new girls who could bring in more money, the older ones were often kicked out—forced to fend for themselves on the street. In some cases, they'd be sold to a lesser brothel, where the number of customers could actually be much higher. I met girls who had been seeing up to thirty men a day. One of them stated, 'I lay there with my eyes closed and my legs spread open. They kept coming, one after another, after another. I lost track of who I was, what I was, where I was. I was simply a piece of meat to be used by those men.'

By her mid-to-late-teens, she would have a body that would be completely ravaged by the effects of disease, alcohol, drugs, and poor nutrition. If she was lucky, she'd somehow make it back to Nepal and to a shelter. Because of the shame she had endured, the idea of facing her family was not a possibility.

For most of these young girls I encountered, their stories ended in death from an AIDS-related illness.

As I continued to visit these shelters, I heard the same themes of horror over and over again. I remember one fifteen-year-old girl telling me she was raped over 7,000 times. She described that each sexual act she was forced to commit was against her will. This was rape. She was raped on schedule, 3,650 times a year. She did this for two years until she was forced to leave because she was suffering from a range of diseases that turned customers away. I remember this girl repeatedly asking me, 'How can a fifteen-year-old girl be raped 7,000 times without anyone doing something to help? How can this happen?' Even after thirty-six years, I still don't have an answer to this question. And she is just one of the thousands of girls in the same situation.

Some of the stories these victims told were so horrific that they would make the hair on the back of my neck stand up. I am still haunted by them. I listened to these stories more than thirty years ago, but the situation is still very much the same in Mumbai, throughout other parts of India, and the world.

If it hadn't been for the AIDS epidemic, we probably wouldn't have known anything about these human rights abuses. Until then, most people looked at prostitutes as criminals or bad girls, morally deficient people who were

somehow less than human. Few people ever bothered to go
up to them to hear their stories. The idea that they could be
victims was never considered. But with each tale, the truth
of their suffering was revealed, and people like me came to
understand that this was a tragic human rights abuse that
urgently needed to be addressed. When we pointed the
spotlight on other locations around the world, we came to
realize that what we were seeing went well beyond Nepal and
India; in fact, it existed within prostitution all over the world.
In time, this understanding led to the creation of the counter-
trafficking movement.

A series of tragic circumstances

The plight of these girls was not entirely new to me. During
the time I was getting my master's degree in New York City,
I spent nearly two years volunteering at an adolescent, multi-
service centre called The Door. This facility offered a range
of services to young people, including healthcare, counselling,
vocational training, recreational options, educational tutoring,
and legal services. My role was to provide reproductive
health counselling to those seeking this service. For people
who needed additional assistance, I acted as their primary
case officer.

   While working at this facility, I encountered a dozen or
more young women in prostitution—mostly 'streetwalkers.'
A pimp would have introduced nearly all of them into this
trade. One story that I heard repeatedly went like this:
a teenage girl from a broken family would get into a big
argument with her mother or father. After storming out of
the house, she would board a bus or train with the intent
of running away. Hours later, she would have arrived alone

in New York City with no money and no idea what to do next.

Invariably, a pimp would be scouting the station for a vulnerable-looking girl to arrive. Very quickly, he would approach and befriend her. Initially, he would shower his victim with the things most lacking in her life—love and affection. Then, for a week or two, he would woo her with warmth, attention, food, clothing, money, and a place to stay. He would go to great lengths to make every moment with him positive and supportive. In this way, he'd manipulate and groom the victim to grow more and more dependent on him.

Once the pimp judged that the girl had been sufficiently groomed, he would transition her into prostitution. Sometimes he would tell her that earning money demonstrated the extent of her love and devotion to him. In this case, 'loyalty' was the hook. At other times, he would create a drug addiction and make the girl sell herself in order to earn her 'fix.'

In still other cases, the pimp would threaten to inform her family and friends that she was a prostitute. The potential shame and embarrassment were often enough to convince her to continue. Once she crossed over the line into prostitution, the pimp would generally replace his love and affection with violence and threats. By this point, the girl would feel that she had no way to escape her situation.

I also encountered several examples of young people losing control of their lives through another set of circumstances that eventually led to human trafficking. I provided counselling to a fifteen-year-old Korean American honour student. When I first met her, she was doing great at school. She had amazing grades, played varsity badminton, and excelled in every aspect of her high school experience. Then, it all changed. She met an older boy, fell in love, and things began to fall apart.

She started taking drugs, her grades dropped, she quit all extracurricular activities, and eventually she was thrown out of her house by her parents. To support her drug habit, she began selling herself. Having entered this world, she eventually ended up with a pimp who held her in place with debt and threats. I was shocked at how fragile life can be, and I've never forgotten her tragic story.

My work in New York City showed me how criminals tricked and deceived these girls. None of the young girls I met claimed to have woken up one day, saying, 'When I grow up, I want to be a prostitute.' I often wondered why people showed such little sympathy for their situation. At that time in my life, the terminology of human trafficking had not been created, but looking back, it was slavery. This process continues today, as it has for years.

Hitting close to home

With each such story I heard, I realized this danger can harm any family. In fact, it nearly happened in mine.

Dora was a pretty twenty-three-year-old woman travelling from Germany to meet her husband, who had gone ahead to get settled in Los Angeles, California. The long, lonely boat trip was over, and in New York City she boarded the train for California. When the train stopped in Chicago, she got off, thinking she had reached Los Angeles. She asked people around her, 'Am I here? Have I reached California?' No one could understand her German. She was frantic.

A young, German-speaking man saw her on the train platform and, in response to her questions, assured her that she had arrived in California. He told her that her husband had asked him to escort her to their beautiful new home.

As she was leaving with this stranger, another German couple saw what was happening, took her away from him, and got her back on the train.

Dora was my grandmother. My mother told me this story of how she had nearly been kidnapped in the early twentieth century. The German-speaking man was what people used to refer to as a 'white slaver.' Had my grandmother gone with him, she would have been taken to a brothel in the city and forced into prostitution. For their kindness, the couple who helped my grandmother eventually became godparents to my oldest sister, Julie.

The first time my mother told me this, I was only five years old. At a very young age, I had a habit of wandering off to places a child should not visit unattended. One of these places was Cedar Mountain, a forested area that was five minutes from my home. My mother found a pile of lava rocks I had collected from this mountain hidden under a bush in front of our house. When asked if I knew where they came from, I said no. She knew I was lying. In order to help me understand that there were bad people in this world, she told me my grandmother's story. It had a great impact on my life. From an early age, I understood that deceitful people walked the Earth, and they tricked others out of their freedom. I was frightened by this reality. I realized, even as a child, that had my grandmother gone with this person, my mother and I would not exist.

In this way, I began to understand how slavery harmed people—it robbed them of the future they could have had. Entire lives were stolen away just when they were getting started. All too often, a victim's hopes, dreams, and aspirations vanished beyond hope of recovery. And, as I was to learn, this was only the beginning of how slavery ravaged its victims.

Chapter 2

Inside the Brothels

I didn't understand the extent of this evil until I investigated some of the sex houses myself a few years later. At the invitation of the Indian government, I went into Mumbai brothels to observe the public health conditions. The name of the area was Kaamathipura. It was one of the largest red-light districts in all of Asia. At the time, it was estimated that there were up to 25,000 women and girls working in prostitution in Kaamathipura. The local authorities explained to me that many of them were victims of sex trafficking, made vulnerable as a result of poverty and lack of access to resources and opportunities. My job was to go from brothel to brothel to determine if condoms were being used, and whether or not simple information on HIV/AIDS and other sexually transmitted infections was available. To ensure my safety, a local police officer accompanied me.

A visual sketch of a brothel

Most brothels I visited had a basic layout, so the inspection routine became familiar quickly. I'd walk up a steep set of narrow steps to the first floor. There would be a large parlour where the women and girls spent most of their waking hours waiting for customers. There would usually be five or six prostitutes lounging around in various states of undress, always on display, like wares in a retail store. Often, the parlour would be colourful, the walls painted yellow, with red velvet couches lined along each wall.

Near the back of the parlour, located in a small brick cubbyhole, would often be a shrine containing several brightly coloured prints depicting the gods Ganesh and Kali. There might also be small brass statues of Lakshmi, the goddess of wealth, covered with red powder from early morning *pujas*. Incense burned throughout the day in devotion to these deities and in supplication for protection and favour.

Standing around the brothels were the *goondas*, who offered security and acted as the bouncers for the brothels, making sure all customers paid. Those I met were cruel and sadistic, disciplining the girls when they stepped out of line and taking pleasure in their duties. They were part of an extended network of organized crime that permeated through the entire red-light district, with illicit drugs and trafficked girls.

Vendors circulated freely throughout the corridors, offering alcohol, tea, cigarettes, and snacks. As I walked through the houses, I was struck by the number of people coming and going at any given time.

The girls came from all over India and nearby countries; but disproportionately, most victims came from Nepal. There were many reasons for this. First, because so many of them were naive and uneducated, they could be easily tricked and deceived into leaving their communities. Second, because of the dire poverty they came from, a madam could often get a girl for little money. Third, Nepalese hill girls often had light skin—throughout much of Asia, this feature is considered beautiful. Fourth, it was said that Nepalese girls would take off their clothes more readily than Indian girls, who would simply pull up their saris to offer sex—many customers wanted to have sex with a naked woman. I heard this statement several times from different shelter managers who indicated that the Indian prostitutes were more modest and conservative. Even if they were asked to remove their clothes, they would not do so. In contrast, when the Nepalese girls were told to do something, they were more compliant to avoid punishment.

Fifth, Nepalese hill girls had East Asian facial features, which were considered exotic. Finally, because they were so far from home, the possibility of them running off and getting back was highly unlikely.

A man might hire a girl for as little as ten minutes. No matter how much or little money customers had in their pockets, an arrangement could nearly always be made. Sex buyers with little cash were serviced in a large common room directly behind the parlour. Around a dozen mattresses lay on the floor of this room. These were set aside for sexual acts to take place. Often, each mattress was separated from the others by only a tattered set of white curtains.

To provide some semblance of privacy, this sex room would be kept dark with only one tiny light in the far corner. Otherwise, little concealed the naked couples from anyone looking into the room, as the fans blew the curtains from side to side. With barely enough space on these mattresses for two people to lie down together, the sex play would often spill over into the next 'booth,' whether someone else was in it or not.

At peak times during the evening, each of these mattresses would be occupied. Grunts and groans resonated throughout the room as a kind of assembly-line sex marathon went into full production. During the hot summer months, the rooms could reach a sweltering 30°C. Even with fans whirring noisily at full speed, the heat generated from the physical activity kept the place blistering hot, reeking with the stench of sweat and body odour.

Men stood in line outside this room, waiting for their turn. The customers were provided with old and tattered European porn magazines for their entertainment while they waited. If they became excited early, visits with the girls would be quick. A fast turnover of clients was key to keeping the profits high.

There was often a small toilet near the rear of the building. Despite being cleaned every morning, the bathrooms always smelled of vomit and urine. The only other room on the floor would usually be an office for the brothel's madam. Throughout the day, she kept close tabs on all the money, the clients, and the girls. These offices generally had a small window opening onto the parlour. Through this, the madam watched everything that went on. At any given time, she'd know exactly where her girls were, whom they were with, and when their sessions would end. If a client was taking too long, she would send one of her *goondas* over to get him to pay more or leave. As beyond horrific and surreal as this setup seems, I encountered such brothels time and again in India.

Recognizing that a great deal of money was being generated from the sale of girls and contraband, the landlords who rented out these buildings charged exorbitant fees. Because the red-light district was confined to this area, most of the 3,000-odd buildings in the area were dilapidated. The landlords had no incentive to offer the needed repairs. As a result, safe drinking water and sanitation were scarce. Many of the rooms had leaking walls and ceilings, which allowed mold and mildew to thrive. The buildings were also infested with rats and cockroaches.

At the back of the parlour, behind a large, iron-reinforced door, might be another staircase leading to a second floor. This door was kept locked in an effort to slow down the police during their periodic raids. The second floor was usually set aside for those customers who were willing to pay for more privacy and a longer stay with a particular girl.

These upper floors frequently contained a dozen small rooms, each no more than one by two metres in size. Apart from a single wicker bed that took up much of the space, there was no other furniture in them. The walls of many of these rooms were covered with an assortment of faded movie star posters and pictures from magazines and newspapers. Some rooms might have had air conditioners for those who could afford a premium rate. Other rooms had small ceiling fans for ventilation.

Girls who had been in the brothels for several years were sometimes allowed to sleep in these rooms. It was one of the few perks offered to those who cooperated. Since there were many more sex providers than beds, newcomers had to sleep on the mattresses in the common room. Four or five prostitutes could often be seen sleeping together on the same mattress. When they were done with their shift, they would join the others. If all the mattresses were taken, they slept on the floor, wherever they could find a free spot.

Throughout much of the day, the tiny rooms on the second floor were filled with customers coming and going.

After the madam set the price for a client, the designated girl would escort him upstairs. The price of having sex in one of these rooms ran to nearly three times more than what it would cost to use a mattress in the common area on the first floor. Any day, depending on client flow, a girl might see between six and twelve customers over a sixteen-hour period.

This was the world many girls had to endure for years. I still have nightmares about those brothels. Memories of the blank stares in the girls' eyes and the feelings of despair that consumed those awful places still haunt me. I can't imagine hell would be much different than what I observed there.

Without what happened next, I might still have shaken off the things I had seen, or at least handled them less obsessively, despite all my previous exposure to the world of human trafficking. I wasn't one of those fifteen-year-old high school kids who wanted to be an activist and save the world. I had other plans for my life. I wanted to have a stellar career with the US Government. I didn't want to get involved in a cause. Other interests awaited me once my work in Mumbai ended. There was no way to expect the following life-defining encounter.

Activist beginnings

At one of the brothels, upon entering the waiting area, an eleven-year-old Nepalese trafficking victim saw me and ran up to me. She wrapped her arms around my waist, and in Nepalese she said, 'Save me, save me, they are doing terrible things to me!'

I looked down in shock at this young girl. She had straight black hair cut in a simple hanging style that reached her shoulders. A dress, ten sizes too big, hung on her small frame.

She had a pre-adolescent body. This was a child in an adult world. I can never forget the pleading desperation in her light-brown eyes.

I turned to the police officer and said, 'We need to take this girl out of here, now.'

'No, we can't do that,' he said.

'Why not? You're a cop!'

'Because they will kill us before they will let us leave with her. Finding a child this age will create a lot of problems for them.'

We left, frustrated, but returned several hours later with more police officers. The officer I was with had to convince these others to act. It took some persuading. I felt they resisted because it would add more work to their shift.

When we arrived back, the young girl was gone. While the officers did a thorough job searching every floor, she was never found. Because of the severe fines and penalties that a brothel could face with such a young victim, they had presumably moved her to another location.

I will never know what happened to that precious child, but I am sure it included beatings, torture, and a drastically shortened life full of misery. Almost certainly, that little girl is long dead now—someone so young in the brothels had a very high probability of contracting HIV and dying of AIDS.

Every once in a while, each of us is given a life test. This was mine, and I failed. I should have found a way to get that girl out of that awful place, and I couldn't. I failed her so thoroughly that I never even learned her name.

For weeks after encountering this child, I had traumatic nightmares. I was haunted by the desperate expression etched across her face, along with those pleading eyes looking up at me. I would wake up in a cold sweat with my heart pounding in my chest. During these times, I imagined the things I could have done to help her. I could have simply picked her up and ran down the stairs. I could have had the police officer leave and come back with more officers while I stayed at the brothel. There were many other options that came to my mind. The fact that I failed to do these things weighed heavily on my heart.

I also started reflecting on my own life. I had been doing public service work for years, but I finally came to realize that, to a certain extent, I had been doing the work for me—to promote Matt Friedman's career, and get the next big job. It took this terrible situation to bring me back to what it was all about. It wasn't about me. It was about the people out there who needed help.

Not knowing what else to do, I finally surrendered. I accepted the fact that, knowing what I did about this problem, I could no longer turn away. I had to step up and become fully involved. At that moment, an activist was born. Many people who fight this injustice have a similar story to tell. The reality of the pain and suffering gets under a person's skin. Once absorbed, there is no escaping it.

In an attempt to restore some small shred of the dignity stolen from her, I call this child Amulya, which in Nepalese means 'priceless'. Amulya and those like her have an intrinsic worth beyond measure. To give her suffering some meaning, I tell Amulya's story in the hope that others will do what they can to protect women and girls around the world from similar fates.

The best way to understand the extent of an issue is through the eyes of a person who has experienced it. A few months after my encounter with Amulya, I started visiting shelters in Nepal that took in rescued trafficking victims.

At a shelter in Kathmandu, I met a young girl named Meena. She had been trafficked to India and endured the brothels for several years. She had AIDS. The next day, I received a letter from her. The depth of Meena's anguish can be felt in her words. Read these words carefully—they hold a very important message.

Matthew,

Thank you for your kindness in coming to see me yesterday at the shelter. Your words brought great joy to my broken heart.

I turn fifteen on Monday. After being used by so many men, I can see that my days will soon come to an end. My illness gets worse with each passing day. I can hardly eat. The food has no flavour. It is sour, like so much of my life. I will not see my sixteenth birthday.

I look back on that day when I left my family's home. I was only twelve then. I was so happy. So full of life. I had such hopes and dreams. Now look at me. I will never marry. I will never have children. I will never have grandchildren. I will not grow old.

The day that first man took my virtue was the day my God died. He and all those other men stole my life away. I was just a child. Why did nobody come to help me? I have stopped asking why this happened to me. I have even stopped feeling angry.

I need you to promise me. I need you to do what you can to prevent any other girls from falling into this hole. Promise me you will end this evil. Promise me you will never stop trying. I don't care about myself. I'm done. Don't let any more of our sisters go through what I went through.

My spirit is already dead inside. My body will soon catch up. How can this happen to a child? Where are all the good men? Where are our protectors? Where is our humanity? Promise me.

Meena

I read and re-read this letter at least twenty times that day, with tears streaming down my face. Many of us who work in this field are driven by these passionate pleas. Many other victims have similar thoughts and feelings that are never revealed to the world. This offers us a glimpse into their broken hearts.

Meena was only fifteen years old. She was commercially raped more than 7,000 times. There are literally millions of women and girls in this situation. She asked two important questions: 'Where are all of the good men? Where are our protectors?' They are out there. We just need to find them, wake them up, and help them to work alongside us to combat this problem.

After leaving Nepal to relocate to Bangladesh, I never returned to this shelter. Several years later, I heard from one of my colleagues that Meena had passed. This was the fate of so many of these girls. To add insult to injury, after having their lives taken away from them, after being forced to be with all of these men, their final outcome was death.

Reading this letter so many years ago was another epiphany that helped me understand that we have a mandate to help end the suffering of those like Meena. Human trafficking represents one of the most disgusting human rights violations of our time. To truly address this problem, I realized that we needed to establish a second-generation abolitionist movement in which we all step up and do our part.

Abolitionists who changed history

English abolitionist William Wilberforce and others led the first movement 180 years ago. Over a seventeen-year period, Wilberforce fought tirelessly to end the slave trade. This effort began in 1789 in Britain, with a three-hour speech against slavery that he presented to the Parliament. Two years later, he presented a bill to the House of Commons to significantly reduce the slave trade and make it unprofitable, which eventually passed. Years later, in 1807, he was able to convince the Parliament to completely abolish the slave trade. For many, Wilberforce represents the symbol of what it means to be an abolitionist.

Between 1830 and 1870, there were five abolitionists in the USA who were often credited with ending slavery: Frederick Douglass, Harriet Beecher Stowe, Sojourner Truth, Harriet Tubman, and John Brown.

Each of these people helped in raising awareness about the issue and bringing about changes needed to end slavery. For this reason, they represent heroes for us to learn from as we address human trafficking in our own time.

We can do the same again today. For human trafficking to end, we must care. We all must care.

For some, a desire to act when confronted with injustice is programmed into their DNA. For others, it needs to be encouraged and nurtured. The people who experience these violations continue to ask the world, 'Where are you? Why are you not helping us?' These are reasonable and legitimate questions to ask.

When you read the stories above, how did they affect you? Did you feel a desire to help? Were these feelings strong enough to bring about a change in you? Hold on to these thoughts— we will delve deeper into this topic later in the book.

Chapter 3

Child Trafficking

Because of the deep moral repugnance of having a child in a situation in which they are forced to have sex with adults, I feel it is worth adding some additional details to shed light on this important topic. This chapter builds upon the previous content by delving deeper into some of the experiences I had related to this horrific problem.

After my initial visits to the Mumbai red-light district, I soon discovered that other brothels in India harboured one or two pre-teen girls. Some of them were less than ten years old and would live on the upper floors in rooms protected by a reinforced door.

Myths related to having sex with children

To my horror, I learned that pedophiles weren't the only men interested in having sex with young children. Others held delusions that sex with very young girls would cure diseases such as gonorrhea or syphilis. Some believed that they could not catch diseases such as AIDS by having sex with someone so young and seemingly healthy. In reality, the opposite often happened. Since the vaginas of these girls were so small and lacked natural lubrication, intercourse often resulted in tears in the vaginal tissues, which significantly increased their chances of becoming infected and diseased. And some men thought that sex with a child would rejuvenate their virility, as if the girl's youth would be transferred on to them. For these reasons, the brothels highly valued their prostituted children, but only until they turned twelve or so, and only as long as they remained healthy.

Unspeakable crimes against children

I also learned that some children were drugged and unconscious during the first dozen of their sexual encounters. The standard rate for sex with a 'child virgin' was sometimes more than half the entire price paid to buy the child. One brothel boasted that a handful of rich Arab businessmen were willing customers in these exchanges, providing windfall profits to the brothel owners. There was even an arrangement made, that if a new child was brought in, the businessmen would fly from the Middle East to spend a weekend.

Because of the potential legal difficulties associated with keeping child sex slaves in brothels, these girls were isolated most of the time, seldom coming in contact with others. If caught and charged by the authorities, the brothel owner could receive up to twenty years in jail, along with a very stiff fine. When a child sex slave would be found, however, arrests almost never occurred. The police could demand enormous bribes for turning a blind eye. The financial burden to the brothel madam could be tremendous.

It is important to note that this situation can be found throughout much of Asia. There is often an informal relationship between the police and those who run the brothels. Because of the high profits generated from prostitution, there is a lot of money that can be used to bribe the police and other authorities for ignoring these businesses. Without a sustained commitment from political leaders, there is little accountability and oversight of this illegal activity.

To protect the brothel from exorbitant fees, secret compartments were built beside each of the children's beds for them to hide in during police raids. The girls were regularly made to practice climbing quickly and quietly into these compartments. Only the madam and a few others knew of their existence.

Through beatings and other forms of physical or emotional abuse, the police were adept at persuading the regular prostitutes to reveal their brothel's secrets. To ensure the children hid during raids, the madams frightened them with exaggerated stories about the police, telling them the officers were horrible monsters who would do terrible things to them if they ever got caught. The girls believed everything the madam said, often becoming hysterical after each raid and clinging to the woman who acted as a perverse sort of surrogate mother.

The police would always be looking for ways to extort more money from the madams, sometimes sending plainclothes officers inside as customers. Knowing this, the madams were very selective in who they allowed to pay for sex with the children, often only accepting referrals from long-time, trusted customers.

During my visits to the Mumbai brothels, I never observed any of these very young children who had been forced into prostitution. Most brothel owners were careful enough to ensure that if either strangers or the police entered the building, steps would immediately be taken to ensure that they would not be found. But on a few occasions, I observed a child's toy in a brothel room under a bed. It is still hard for me to fathom that a prepubescent girl could be playing with a doll one minute, and then be forced to have sex with an adult a few minutes later. What kind of evil allows this to happen? I'll never understand this.

The more I came in contact with this crime against humanity, the more I wanted to do something—anything—to help. After encountering Amulya and so many others who suffered like her, I grew desperate to find a way to contribute. Realizing that few people around the world in the 1990s knew anything about the problem, I decided to write a book that would help the public truly understand the atrocities taking place. From the beginning, I knew I needed an approach that would stand apart from the impersonal, academic studies on the subject. Research papers never captured the true essence of what was involved when a person was forced into prostitution. Most people don't read dry, scholarly documents in any case.

I decided to try to describe what happens through the medium of fiction. I sought to develop an understanding of the problem, and possibly some empathy, by depicting characters who experienced trafficking as the story unfolded. I felt this would allow readers to understand the problem, not only on an intellectual level, but also an emotional one.

This type of storytelling represents a traditional form of communication that has existed from the beginning of time. There is something about a story that ties a series of events, actions, and outcomes together in a way that provides true clarity and profound meaning. We relate to stories because our lives are made up of them. Whenever we describe an event in our own lives, we often use storytelling to do so. In this way, the story as a form of expression is very familiar to all of us. Using this approach can be an effective means of shedding light on the situation, which can compel readers to step up and get involved.

Exposing the evil of human trafficking

The first book I wrote was titled *Tara: A Fleshtrade Odyssey*. Before penning the manuscript, I asked people what they would be willing to read on the topic. They said they liked the idea of a novel. They felt that having characters to relate to would make the story more real. But, they also said it couldn't be too graphic or else they wouldn't finish it.

Armed with this information, I wrote the book, and it was published in 1997. While it did well among the general public, the counter-trafficking community did not like it at all. They said my nuancing of the horrors of human trafficking was a disservice. They felt the story should have gone into great detail about the pain and suffering these women and girls endured. I couldn't argue with this critique. It was true that I had watered down the graphic elements of the story. I did this in the hope that more people would read the book.

Feeling that I might have gotten it all wrong, I decided to write a second book, one that would encapsulate the most heart-wrenching details. I called it *Captive Daughters*. Although it has been finished for many years, predictably, no one has been willing to publish it. The detailed accounts of the rapes and torture scenes were considered too graphic for both publishers and readers because I held nothing back.

While many people have encouraged me to tone down the text, I couldn't do it. During my interviews for the book, the girls asked if I'd be presenting the graphic details of their encounters. When I told them that I might have to water them down, nearly all of them said they would not allow me to use their story if I did. They felt it was essential for the reader to understand the full extent of the horror they had experienced. To honour their wishes, I have kept the text as it is. Not publishing this manuscript has been one of my biggest regrets in life. For many years, I was convinced that if this story was told, more people would wake up and care about the plight of these victims. I was never able to validate this theory.

Someday, I hope to revisit the process of publishing this manuscript. Even after all these years, many of the stories I conveyed in this novel are still very relevant. They still need to be told.

To collect the information I needed for *Captive Daughters*, I visited a range of shelters located in Nepal. The women who ran them were people who had absolute dedication to these victims—offering them a place to stay, along with food, healthcare, counseling, job training, and a chance to recover. Whenever possible, they also helped girls to return home. For most, however, this was not an option. The families had been the ones who trafficked them in the first place, or wouldn't accept them back because they felt that their daughter brought shame and dishonour to the household.

Where were you?

While nearly all of the girls I approached agreed to tell me their personal stories, one fifteen-year-old named Gita repeatedly declined my requests for an interview. Every time

I approached her, she withdrew angrily. But, during all of my interviews in her shelter, she sat off to one side and listened to everything being said.

On the last day of my visit to this shelter, Gita finally came up to me and said she had changed her mind; she would give me an interview. Everyone was surprised. I thanked her and asked her to sit down on one side of the table. Three other shelter staff sat on the other side with me.

Over the next three hours, Gita described one of the most gut-wrenching testimonials I have ever heard. It was filled with deception, rape, torture, murder, disease, and so much more. It seemed to me that she had suffered the worst of everything times ten. Having spoken with hundreds of other girls, I thought I had heard everything. But this description was almost beyond belief.

At the end of the interview, I sat there speechless. After an extended pause, I thanked Gita for sharing her astonishing story. There was another pause. Her eyes had this piercing gaze, full of a combination of pain, sorrow, and anger. I couldn't distinguish which emotion was the most prevalent. Not knowing what else to do, I finally said, 'Wow, you must be so angry at the traffickers for all of the terrible things they did to you.' I then waited for her confirmation of this seemingly obvious statement.

Instead, Gita looked accusingly at me and the others in the room. Her eyes blazed. 'No, I am not angry at the traffickers— I am angry at *you*!' she shouted, pointing her finger at each of us in turn. 'Where were you when I was in that terrible brothel? I sat in that place every day, waiting for someone to come and save me. I knew that everything happening around me was illegal and wrong. I went to school until I was twelve. I knew it was slavery. Where were *you* and everyone else when

I needed you?' She paused and took a few deep breaths. Tears began falling from her face.

'Why are you sitting here?' she added. 'Why aren't you down there, helping my sisters? They are in the same situation I was in. Everyone knows what is going on. Everyone knows it is wrong. Why is no one helping them? How can such terrible things happen without anyone doing anything? I am not angry with the traffickers. They are just bad people doing what they do—bad things. I am angry at the good people, society, you! WHERE WERE YOU? Where was everyone? Why did no one help? Why does no one care?'

The fundamental question

That day, a survivor spoke for herself and for so many others. She called us all out, asking the fundamental question: 'Why doesn't the world care enough to stop this crime against humanity?' It was a profoundly relevant question then, and remains so today.

That moment was an epiphany that helped me understand that we, the citizens of the world—collectively and individually—have a responsibility to address this problem. Whether the victims of trafficking are in India, Nepal, China, Africa, Latin America, the United States, or anywhere else, human trafficking shreds the fabric of all that is good and decent in this world. It is not someone else's problem. It belongs to each of us.

The same can be said for other social issues too. Whether it be poverty, environmental stewardship, or violence against women, we must all understand that our failure to act contributes to these social problems. As Ginetta Sagan, a well-known human rights activist who fought injustices in Europe following WWII once said, 'Silence in the face of injustice is complicity with the oppressor.'

Over the years, my encounter with Gita has been one of my signature stories. Her final plea to us was so startling, that it forced me to stop and think about my own value system and ethics. Sometimes the people we least expect to understand this world of ours can teach us all important lessons. Gita made me take a step back and look at where we are.

Chapter 4

The Counter-Trafficking Community

As a result of these experiences, I devoted much of my time to helping the fight against human trafficking. My journey began and continued in Nepal. There, I spent eight years learning about the problem, experimenting with different approaches, and finding out what worked and what didn't work. This included raising funds for shelters, developing a multi-stakeholder committee that included NGOs and UN officials, supporting movie projects to raise awareness, collecting data on human trafficking trends, providing training, and offering help to rescued victims. At this time, there was limited literature available on this issue. I once found a thirty-page brochure that had been published by a little-known Christian charity, and I read and re-read this publication over and over again. It helped me to validate some of my own observations.

In these early years (1991-1997), the biggest challenge we faced was convincing people that the plight of these women and girls was a human rights issue. Much of society looked at those in prostitution as 'bad girls' or criminals. It wasn't until the HIV/AIDS epidemic hit that anyone paid attention to them. After development workers like myself offered our public health information to these women, we started asking questions about how they got into the business. It was only then that the terrible stories emerged. Many of us were shocked by what we heard. At first, we didn't know what to do with this information because it wasn't a health issue. The human rights groups were also at a loss—the topic didn't seem to fit well under any development category.

HIV/AIDS and human trafficking

During this time, as the number of HIV/AIDS cases continued to soar, various NGO groups began to get involved. This included the development of shelters, community prevention programmes, legal support initiatives, policy development efforts, and more. Since much of this early work took place in Nepal, the country soon distinguished itself as a leader in the counter-trafficking movement.

Until 1997, I returned to Washington, D.C. every summer to offer a briefing on our country's programme. While I was there, I'd tell my co-workers about this 'new' issue. I would go on and on about the people I had met who were trapped in this enslaved condition. I am sure I irritated those who had grown tired of hearing my relentless ranting. On more than a few occasions, I would walk into a cafeteria or a reception hall and watch as people I knew pretended not to see me while making their escape. Although my feelings were often hurt, I felt I had to continue to educate and inform them. This was the only way we could have had a breakthrough.

I once walked into a meeting where the Director said to me, 'You can say all you want about the topic of human trafficking, but you're not getting any HIV/AIDS money from us to help. So don't bother asking.' After telling several stories, I walked out of that meeting with a commitment for $100,000—my first such success. That was a good day. What did I say to bring about this outcome? I told the group that those who are trafficking and selling people have no regard for their victims' personal health or safety. For this reason, they are less likely to ensure that condoms are being used to prevent HIV/AIDS. Thus, an investment in addressing human trafficking can help reduce HIV/AIDS.

The US government steps up to help

In 1998, everything changed. The Clinton administration decided that human trafficking was an important human rights issue. At the Association of Southeast Asian Nations conference, the US Secretary of State Madeline Albright declared that the US government intended to put in place a major international programme to help address this worldwide issue of slavery. Three years later, the US State Department became the world's largest anti-trafficking player. Around the same period, other governments joined the global effort, including those of Australia, Canada, Norway, and the UK.

Within a short time, I went from being almost completely ignored to being sought after for my expertise. It was one of those strange times in life when it felt like a switch had been flipped. There was one particular day when this sudden change almost seemed surreal. I had finished a series of public health briefings at the USAID headquarters building in Washington, D.C. Discouraged by the previous reactions people had had with my attempts to initiate interest in human trafficking, I decided not to bring up the topic this time around. I didn't have the energy to face the anticipated disappointment. As I was about to leave, one of my colleagues asked if I was still doing any counter-trafficking work. When I reluctantly responded with a yes, several people came up to me and asked, 'Do you really know about that topic? Can we talk to you about this? We've been asked to do research for the Director, but we don't know where to begin.' With the entire group taking copious notes, the conversation that followed lasted several hours.

While donor money began to flow, little was set aside for research or data collection. One donor representative stated, 'We don't have time to gather that information. We need to go out and help these poor people.' This same trend has been followed ever since. We still don't have the information we need in order to fully understand the problem.

Those who made a difference

By far, the most influential person in my counter-trafficking career has been Anuradha Koirala. I met her for the first time in the early 1990s, when I was just learning about this topic. The first time we met, she arrived at my office on the back of a motorcycle. She came to me looking for support for a human trafficking shelter she had recently set up. Having received three US government containers filled with medical supplies from military bases that had closed down across Asia, I was able to provide her with beds, mattresses, and many other useful items. From that point forward, we became friends.

Prior to becoming an activist, Anuradha had been teaching children at various schools across Kathmandu for twenty years. In 1993, a friend came to her and asked if she could take in a girl in her home who had been trafficked into the brothels in India. Little did she know that this event would completely change the course of her life. After hearing the girl's story, something about this issue really triggered a sense of justice. After that, she continued to take in more and more girls. She had found her calling, and within a short time, she had become an unstoppable force of nature.

While there are many stories I could tell about her work, there is one that really sticks out in my mind. In the early days, before setting up any shelters, there was one girl Anuradha had a connection with, more than most of the others. She loved this girl like a daughter. One day, Anuradha told this girl she had to leave to go to Nepalgunj for a short trip. While she found herself getting more involved in the human trafficking movement, she had not yet crossed over the line to be considered an activist. The girl begged her not to go; she said she was going to die. Anuradha, feeling that the girl was exaggerating what seemed to be a harmless ailment, told her this wouldn't happen, and left. Despite this reassurance, somehow the girl passed away.

Anuradha was completely heartbroken. After going to the cremation site, they told her she'd have to pay ten times more to perform the cremation service because the deceased was considered a 'bad girl.' The fact that this injustice extended even beyond her friend's death had a devastating impact on Anuradha, and she became obsessed with fighting for this cause. From that day onwards, she demonstrated an unrelenting determination to do everything in her power to prevent girls from being trafficked, to bring the criminals to justice, and to offer compassionate support to the victims.

From a small shelter with only a few beds, she has built a large network that includes three prevention homes, eleven transit homes, two hospices, and a formal school. More than a thousand children are receiving direct services from Anuradha's non-profit organization, Maiti Nepal, every day. This was all made possible due to her firm determination and unprecedented leadership.

During my time in Nepal, I visited her shelter countless times to learn about the problem. In fact, many of the stories outlined in this book revolve around her centre and her efforts.

For many years, Anuradha kept risking her life to do this work. During the time I was in Nepal, at least two of her staff were murdered by traffickers. Her life has also been threatened countless times. But despite this danger, she always put her own safety aside to fight for these girls. During my life, I have met a few people who displayed this selfless dedication to those in need. For this reason, she will always be one of my greatest heroes.

The power of film

Another noteworthy activity I participated in was a film documentary project produced by Andrew Levine, a young filmmaker who had heard about the human trafficking issue. He didn't know much about the topic, and he reached out to me through a mutual friend. Since I was in Nepal and he was in Utah, it was hard to communicate. But when he heard I'd be returning to Connecticut to visit my parents over the summer, he flew there to meet me at my home.

We sat and talked for nearly ten hours, and the outcome was a plan to do a film in Nepal. After submitting a proposal to the Gates Foundation, we managed to get the funding we needed. To make the film, Andrew spent several months interviewing the trafficking victims at Maiti Nepal. He also visited several field sites to learn more about the problem. To help the viewers get a glimpse into the brothels, Andrew and his team used spy cameras that were embedded in their glasses. The final product, titled *The Day My God Died*, won many awards and was nominated for an Emmy. If you watch the film, you will see me as a young, very angry activist. Over time, I have toned down my feelings, but back then, I was full of rage.

From Nepal to Bangladesh

From Nepal, I moved to Bangladesh in 1998 and stayed there for nearly five years. There, I had the chance to take the lessons I had learned in Nepal and apply them to a fresh country programme. I also got involved in other regional and country efforts across South Asia, including India and Sri Lanka. It was a period when the four Ps (Prevention, Prosecution, Protection, and Policy) were tried and tested around the world, as described below.

- **Prevention** efforts attempt to ensure that people are not trafficked. This approach focuses on addressing the vulnerabilities of target communities through awareness-raising campaigns, vocational training, microcredit, and programmes to increase access to education for vulnerable children.
- **Prosecution** related activities include the development of specific anti-trafficking laws, and training of police officers, prosecutors and judges to effectively respond to human trafficking.
- **Protection** of trafficking victims has been accomplished through providing a wide range of

services, including medical and psychosocial support, shelter, legal assistance, and support for safe return and reintegration.

- **Policy** and cooperation includes the development and implementation of national plans and policies, as well as mechanisms such as multi-sectoral committees and working groups that strengthen coordination and cooperation within countries and across borders.

Using this paradigm, we learned many important lessons. The building blocks for nationwide programmes were put in place. For example, national 'plans of action' were written, laws were changed, and the whole counter-trafficking movement gained traction.

Forced labour was also beginning to emerge as a relevant issue to the counter-trafficking sector. Although the human trafficking definition addressed forced labour, this was seldom discussed in the early years. Because of the moral repugnance of forced prostitution, I estimate that 95 per cent of the initial response focused on sex trafficking. This trend continued for nearly fifteen years.

There was another trend happening at this time. Two major camps fought to win over the hearts and minds of the counter-trafficking community. One side argued that prostitution, by its nature, was highly exploitative for the prostitutes, damaging to society, and should be ended. This abolitionist group argued if the demand for prostitution could be stopped, trafficking would go away, and society would benefit from the added emphasis on women's rights.

On the other side of the argument stood organizations that fought for the rights of sex workers. They argued that for most, prostitution was a business choice between consenting adults and should be legalized and regulated. They reasoned that an empowered sex industry would push out the criminal element and replace it with a legitimate business model. They pointed to how ending alcohol prohibition in the United States wiped out the illicit market's profits.

Throughout this debate, which became very personal at times, I did my best to walk a path between these two extremes. I felt the issue we were all addressing was so big and so important, we couldn't afford to take any of our energy away from directly addressing the problem. Fighting between the groups became a major distraction. For me, we had enough common ground to justify an alliance. But this never happened. Both sides continue to fight over this issue to this day. Since I walked the middle path, both sides were suspicious of my intentions. This sometimes made the journey very uncomfortable. On at least three occasions, I have been confronted by senior officials who questioned my loyalty to the overall cause.

Controversy permeated the issue of human trafficking during this time period. Once, I was asked to present a paper at a major conference in Hawaii. The US government had such deep reservations over my participation that it sent a senior official to accompany me throughout the conference. She steered me away from many political minefields.

Establishing conceptual clarity

During my time in Bangladesh, a counter-trafficking thematic group gathered forty organizations together in Dhaka to debate, discuss, and theorize about the problem.

The group met every other week over an eighteen-month period. For me, this was one of the most satisfying experiences of my career. Specific topics that were debated and discussed included:

- The need to move beyond sex trafficking to include forced labour as a relevant topic;
- the differences between migration and human trafficking;
- the nexus between human trafficking and the HIV/AIDS sector; and
- the importance of including men as trafficked persons.

During these in-depth discussions, the representatives concluded the following:

- Many trafficking definitions that were in use tended to be limited in their scope and did not reflect the totality of the problem.
- There were many inconsistencies in the existing human trafficking paradigm that were yet to be resolved in Bangladesh.
- The sector still lacked conceptual clarity even among those who were working to reduce the problem.
- There was a need to 'rethink' some of the previous assumptions in order to restructure and revise/expand the understanding of the problem.

From the first day the Thematic Group was formed, the concept of putting in place a 'second generation response' within the trafficking sector was introduced. As a direct result of this approach, the following changes were implemented within the national programme:

- The different trafficking outcomes (e.g. domestic servitude, camel jockeys, beggars, factory workers, and prostitution) were all given equal attention when addressing the trafficking problem;
- new approaches and interventions were identified and used to address the needs of women who have been trafficked versus children who have been trafficked;
- a new theoretical understanding was introduced to resolve the ambiguities and uncertainties concerning migration and trafficking; and
- participation of trafficked persons was introduced at all stages of counter-trafficking interventions.

Bangladesh has a culture that is passionate about taking theory and experience, and debating the merits of an issue's components. The experience taught me the importance of establishing conceptual clarity as the basic foundation for addressing a problem. The process informed and enriched us all. I felt sad leaving Dhaka.

A new chapter in Thailand

My next assignment took me to Bangkok, Thailand, in 2003. There, I became the Deputy Director of the USAID Regional Health office. While the idea of managing regional programmes was initially an attraction for me, I soon began to miss the close contact I enjoyed while working in a country setting. I began to lose momentum in my counter-trafficking work. I had a number of starts and stops that eventually led to a dead end. I experienced a crisis of sorts that put me into a depressive state. I began to lose interest in my work. Things were not good for me at that time.

But in 2005, circumstances changed again. I started to feel a fire for the topic to re-emerge. For a variety of reasons, more and more doors opened spontaneously. There was renewed interest, and, most importantly, funding increased. I entered my own personal Renaissance period.

Managing a United Nations project to fight human trafficking

In 2006, after seventeen years with USAID, I joined the United Nations. On a whim, I applied for a job as the regional project manager for the United Nations Interagency Project on Human Trafficking (UNIAP). To my surprise, I was offered the position. After serious contemplation, I decided to make this monumental move. This resulted in me leaving the relative comfort of the US State Department system to take on a job that paid considerably less, and came with few benefits. But the tradeoff was worth it—I could work on the issue of human trafficking full-time all across Asia. It offered an amazing opportunity.

My responsibilities included offices in China, Cambodia, Laos, Myanmar, Thailand, and Vietnam. At times, I managed a staff of up to forty people. Our role was to work with governments, NGOs and others to find solutions to address human trafficking problems.

At first, the work was satisfying. We did groundbreaking research, brought governments together, funded innovative NGO efforts, and set up a hotline inside the UN complex.

Our staff was highly committed and full of immense talent. I was proud to be managing this programme.

During this period, three trends emerged. First, forced labour began to rise as a major concern within the human trafficking sector and news media. We saw more attention being given to trafficking cases on fishing boats and within sweatshops across the region. Second, the concept of supply chain management within the private sector gained prominence as a solution to the problem. We encouraged companies to monitor their supply chains to the lowest level to help reduce the number of trafficking cases. Third, 'slavery' as a term was beginning to replace 'human trafficking'. Experts in the field argued that slavery put more emphasis on the real problem—the loss of freedom—while human trafficking focused more on the process a victim followed to get into the exploitative situation. The word slavery was also easier to understand for many and offered a more emotive response.

One of my biggest frustrations was finding ways to get the counter-trafficking community to collaborate. While some groups did get together to share ideas and participate in joint activities, there were also many occasions where collaboration was lacking due to simple misunderstandings, polarized political views, or a lack of faith in the process of working together. Nevertheless, this lack of cooperation often wasted time and took away from our mandate to help and support those in need. This problem is not unique to the human trafficking sector and can be found in many other humanitarian development settings.

To create true, sustained collaboration between organizations, a foundation of trust and a united sense of purpose needed to be built. If feelings of accomplishment within a collaborative process were developed, joint ownership of the problem often followed. For all of this to happen, organizations needed to create an environment that was positive, supportive, and encouraged innovation from an early stage of the program. This process needed to take place among all sectors—between governments, the UN and bilateral partners, non-profit and community-based organizations, and the private sector—to develop a comprehensive, sustained response that could cater to the needs of the entire community. The key to a successful collaboration was a strategic collaboration, not a tokenistic one. Addressing this need was a big part of our ongoing work.

Lessons from roadblocks

Over time, elements within the project changed. The UN, like most multinational groups, can become very political. By my fourth year, we faced challenges from within the UN system itself. As a non-UN insider, I didn't always understand the way things worked; and, at times, I learned what I needed to know only after the damage had been done. For example, the UN has what I call the 'five/seven rule.' It goes like this: a UN organization would say that there were five things they wanted to do, but alongside this list were seven reasons why the programme couldn't move forward. As long as everyone had the five/seven rule in place, a balance was maintained, and the donors would say, 'Since everyone is struggling, this work must be very hard. We must give the UN lots of resources and time.'

But we never really understood this concept. When we said we would do five things, we ended up doing seven. While we got excited about our achievements, some of the other agencies grew jealous. We became an irritant when donors would point towards us and say to the other organizations,

'Why don't you become more like UNIAP?' It was the beginning of our downfall. From this experience, I learned not to raise my head above everyone else because it is a good way to get it chopped off. By the sixth year, we were fighting other UN agencies more than the traffickers. For me, it was time to leave, or rather, be pushed out.

Despite the issues we faced, it was a fantastic learning experience. My biggest lessons have always come from the greatest obstacles and failures I have faced. I had a lot of both. But despite the fact the process nearly sucked the life out of me, I managed to leave without any poison in my heart. I forgave my foes and repaired as many bridges as I could. I moved on.

As my exposure to this issue continued to grow, so did my ability to quantify the problem. Modern slavery, which represents the recruitment, transport, receipt, and harbouring of people for the purpose of exploiting their labour, affects almost all parts of the world. Globally, it is estimated that there are over 40 million men, women, and children in situations of modern slavery today. These victims, who can be found in factories, construction sites, fisheries, and sex venues, are forced to work for little or no pay, deprived of their freedom, and often subjected to unimaginable suffering.

While most people think that human trafficking focuses primarily on women and girls being forced into the sex industry, this represents only about 19 per cent of the total cases. The remaining 81 per cent fall under the heading 'forced labour.' Out of this figure, about 60 per cent of the victims are associated with manufacturing supply chains, which begin with a grower or producer and end as a finished product purchased by consumers in the retail market.

David versus Goliath

The international counter-trafficking community has not come close to meeting its full potential. While individual, small-scale success stories can be found, many victims are never identified. For example, the 2021 Trafficking in Persons Report was only able to account for 109,000 victims receiving assistance globally. This means that less than 0.2 per cent of the victims are being identified and assisted each year. That number has remained unchanged for several years. Even if this figure were doubled, tripled, or quadrupled, it would still be outrageously low. During the same time period, less than 8,000 out of an estimated 500,000 criminals received a conviction.

Why are these numbers so low? The profits generated from this illicit trade were estimated to exceed $150 billion annually, according to a report by the International Labour Organization in 2016. Despite the size of the problem, I know of no scholarly study that attempts to determine how much money is applied to the problem. But one informal report said that donor contributions add up to some $350 million per year. This represents considerably less than one percent of the total profits generated by the criminals. To put this number into perspective, in the United States we eat US$6 billion worth of potato chips annually. It takes twenty-one days of potato chip eating to equal the amount of money that is used globally to address this problem. It is not surprising that the number of trafficked persons continues to soar into the tens of millions. Our response is like taking a slingshot and going after a tank.

Modern slavery and the private sector

As I came to internalize the importance of this data, I began to feel that for the world to make a real difference in addressing this problem, the private sector must become a player. But why should the business world care about this topic? The answer is simple: modern slavery is an ever-increasing business risk. Governments and regulators around the world are clamping down, and companies need to show they have done everything in their power to reduce slavery in their operations, or face condemnation, fines, loss of access to government contracts, and/or prosecution.

Beginning in 2012, a new transparency legislation has been put in place, which requires major companies to indicate what they are doing to address modern slavery. This includes the California Transparency in Supply Chain Act, the UK Modern Slavery Act, France's Duty of Vigilance, and the Australian Modern Slavery Act.

We've seen a significant rise in the number of class action lawsuits against major retail and manufacturing companies within the fishing, chocolate, electronics, and garment industries. When human trafficking conditions are found in a business sector, they can result in an entire industry receiving a bad name.

Modern slavery is now on the radar of the media and NGOs, many of whom are unafraid to publicly shame and thrust brands into the spotlight for failing to address it. There has been a significant increase in investigative journalism and data collection to highlight and expose modern slavery within a range of industries. In some cases, campaigns have been launched to encourage consumers to write to those companies that have been linked with modern slavery.

More and more consumers are asking questions about whether the products they buy are 'slave free'. As part of this trend, millennials are much savvier when it comes to slavery and are using online resources and apps to identify whether they are using products and services from companies that may profit from the enslavement and exploitation of people. In the investment world, there has been a concerted effort to include metrics related to modern slavery within environmental, social and governance (ESG) frameworks.

As these trends continue, more companies will seek to better understand their vulnerability to modern slavery, and there are many people working in the private sector who have come to realize that slave-like conditions are incompatible with good business.

Armed with this information, I began to engage with the private sector in Hong Kong, which seemed like a logical place to start, given its links with major corporate networks across Asia. I had a number of contacts who helped me set up high-level meetings with a range of captains of industry. During these exploratory meetings, I learned that many of these organizations knew very little about either the issue in general or the specific vulnerabilities that existed within their own businesses. And while most had heard about new and existing compliance legislation, few had the detailed information they needed to fully address the spirit of this legislation.

One thing was clear from these talks: while representatives of these businesses were concerned about the problem and wanted to do whatever was needed to help, they didn't feel comfortable working with the United Nations or any NGOs. They felt these organizations couldn't be trusted. As I came in contact with more and more concerned business people, a number of them said, 'Instead of relying on the UN and NGO world, we should set up an organization in Hong Kong ourselves to use the skills and experience of the private sector to identify and stop human trafficking. Business knows how to address bad business.'

The Mekong Club

And so, the Mekong Club was born in Hong Kong. The organization was the first of its kind in Asia that brought together the immense skills and resources of the private sector to offer a business-to-business approach to the problem. The Mekong Club partners worked with experienced anti-slavery field experts to help companies really understand the extent of the problem and how it can adversely affect their businesses. Training programmes were provided for executives, and focused technical assistance was given to compliance and legal officers.

The ultimate goal of the Mekong Club has been to offer the right tools needed for companies to reduce risks of slavery affecting their business in any way. We also work with the private sector to ask the fundamental question, 'What can each business do to play a role in reducing slavery?' More than fifty companies stepped up and joined the fight.

I am presently the CEO of the Mekong Club. I firmly believe that the private sector has the power to significantly reduce the number of cases of human slavery through more detailed supply chain audits and more direct involvement of their leaders.

852 Freedom Campaign

Finally, alongside my work at the Mekong Club, I was also the Co-Founder and a Director of the 852 Freedom Campaign. The 852 in the name represents the country code for Hong Kong. In March 2015, the senior pastor at the International Christian Assembly Church approached me and my wife, Sylvia. He said it was easy to get Christians to worship and seek fellowship, but less easy to get them to apply their faith to a cause of justice. He invited us to do a three-year campaign to use the issue of human slavery as a means of getting people to act.

To begin this process, we began doing presentations and showing movies on the topic. Our approach was simple—to teach people about the issue, and then encourage them to use their God-given skills, abilities, and experiences to play a role in the fight against human slavery. After starting with five volunteers, our platform quickly grew to nearly 400 volunteers. We also had a working collaboration with more than 120 churches, NGOs and other organizations—over half were Chinese churches. We reached more than 20,000 people through fifty-five events in churches, schools and corporations—young and old alike. We also raised nearly US$200,000 for anti-trafficking programmes.

Working with my wife on this project was a meaningful experience. As a couple, we realized that when it came to doing development projects together, we made a great team. This is not always the case when spouses collaborate on a program of this kind.

There have been failures in the many years I have been engaged in anti-slavery work, but there have also been some incredible breakthroughs that can effect change and, I believe, will help to eradicate these atrocities in the time to come. The areas where progress has been made include:

- recognition of the issue across Asia;
- understanding of how to offer preventive messages to protect people from being trafficked;
- increased use of legal remedies to go after the criminals;
- involvement among the business sector; and
- cooperation between and among governments.

Chapter 5

Hearing Victims' Voices

The real experts in understanding human trafficking are not people like me; they are the traffickers and the victims. Having participated in this process, they have a detailed, personal understanding of the crime and how it unfolds. To better comprehend their experiences, it is important to listen to their stories and descriptions. This information helps break down the trafficking experience into its component parts and clarify the techniques and tools used by the perpetrators.

Modern slavery as a concept

When I describe the issue of modern slavery before a large audience, I often notice that many appear bewildered when the word slavery is mentioned. Sometimes they raise their hand and say something like, 'We don't have slavery any more. It was abolished 150 years ago. In the USA, a war was fought over this problem. There are no more slaves.'

This is a misconception. It's hard for people to imagine that there are more than 40 million men, women, and children enslaved today. To put this into perspective, we have more enslaved people across the globe than the entire population of Canada. In fact, the UN indicates there are more slaves in the world today than ever before in history, and slaves can be found in nearly every country in the world. In some nations, the proportion of people suffering in slavery is extremely high. In Mauritania and Uzbekistan, for example, four out of every one hundred people live as modern slaves.

If one assumes a 20 per cent turnover in the number of slaves annually, this means that there are 9.2 million new slaves each year, 25,200 per day, 1,000 an hour, or one every four seconds. Every time I repeat these figures, I am still surprised and shocked. It's simply unacceptable.

Stolen lives

Human trafficking destroys lives. It tears families apart. Men, women, and children are stolen, deceived, or seduced into opportunities that do not exist; instead, they are condemned to lives of enslavement and exploitation. Over the years, I recorded statements from numerous victims I met and interviewed. One of the best ways to quickly understand the complexity and sheer horror of modern slavery is to listen to them. Here are some stories of people who ended up in situations of forced labour:

> *'When I turned eighteen, my family borrowed money and gave it to an employment agency to get me a job overseas. Since there were passports and plane tickets involved, the costs were high. We were excited because we were told I'd be earning*

$120 per month. After the paperwork was done and I completed a one-week training to become a domestic worker, I flew to the country. At first, I was so excited. I was proud that I'd be earning money for my family. But when I got there, everything changed. Nothing they had said at the agency was right. They made me work from 6:00 a.m. to 11:00 p.m. every day. I was never allowed to leave or have any contact with my family. They beat me every time I did something wrong. Since I didn't understand their language, I was forever making mistakes. When the madam of the house was away, her husband would force himself on me. While I tried to stop him, there was nothing I could do. Since they deducted money for everything—my food, boarding, and medicine—my monthly salary was no more than $10. I was a slave in that house. I wanted to die. When the contract was over, and I went home, my family blamed me for everything. The agency said that I was lazy and talked back. But it wasn't so. It wasn't me. Why doesn't anyone believe me?'

– Cambodian victim exploited in Malaysia

'I was only sixteen years old when I was forced onto that fishing boat. I was told that the job was easy and that I'd be paid a good wage. But instead, I ended up working for eighteen hours a day, every day. For food, we ate nothing but fish and rice twice a day. If I got sick or injured, I worked. I had seen others who had fallen ill, and the captain simply threw them over the side of the boat. I still remember their pleas for help as the ocean carried them away to their deaths. I was beaten if I didn't work hard enough, or even if I did. Days often went by with only a few hours of sleep. I was so tired sometimes I felt I'd go crazy. To keep me working, they would force me to take powerful drugs that destroyed my body. When I finally returned

to the port after four years at sea, I was not given any pay. The captain told me that I was an illegal migrant, so he didn't have to give me anything. Having no way to communicate with my family while I was away, my mother and father assumed I was dead. Since they moved away, I don't know how to find them.'

– Cambodian victim exploited in Thailand

'When I was twenty-one years old, I heard that many factories in Thailand offered work along the ocean, peeling shrimp. So I went there. I didn't know which one had work, so I just chose one. The man who managed the factory said I could have a job. We negotiated a salary of $50 a month. For me, this was a huge amount of money. But he said I couldn't leave the factory. I was okay with this. I needed the money, so I agreed. After working eighteen hours a day for nearly two months, I went to the employer and asked for my pay. He smiled and laughed before saying, "I am sorry, I forgot to mention to you that it costs me $54 a month to keep you here and I am only paying you $50. So you owe me money. Until you pay it back, you cannot leave this place." For three years, I was not able to leave. With armed security guards, barbed wire, and high walls, I couldn't escape. None of us could. The more I worked, the more debt I owed. With so much work and nothing in return, my heart was filled with hopelessness and despair. If that fire hadn't brought the authorities, I would never have been able to leave. I lost three years of my life. Gone…stolen from me. Something I can never get back again.'

– Myanmar victim exploited in Thailand

'When I arrived at the construction site, I was so excited. The foreman told me that I could get a good job. While he said he

couldn't pay me for the first three months, I didn't mind. He seemed like a respectable person. Every day I worked from 7:00 a.m. to 7:00 p.m. The work was hard and dangerous, but that was okay. After three months, I went to get my pay. But the foreman told me that I'd have to wait another two months. While I wasn't happy, what else could I do? I borrowed more money from my friends and continued to work. But each time I asked for my wages, I was told the same answer—next month. After twelve months passed, I was desperate. I was heavily in debt and without any money. When I heard that there were others like me, we all got together, and as a group we approached the foreman. This angered him greatly. The next day, a van pulled up, and the police took us all away. The foreman stood there and smiled. It was he who had called them there. At that moment, I could tell that he had never intended to pay any of us. Two weeks later, I was deported. For an entire year, I worked for nothing. For an entire year, I had been a slave.'

– Lao victim exploited in Thailand

From these profiles, one can see several characteristics that are common to modern slavery. Unlike years ago when men, women, and children were rounded up in Africa and forced onto boats with chains and shackles, today's slavery has a completely different dynamic.

Web of deception

The most common approach traffickers use to recruit and secure victims is fraud and deception. About 90 per cent of the cases I have observed fall into this category. Traffickers gain a person's trust and lie about a possible employment or life opportunity. They might offer a young, vulnerable person who is facing hardship and poverty the one thing that seems completely out of reach: a better life, an easier life, or a life that will benefit not only them but their entire family. They offer a dream, with little or nothing asked for in return.

Whether such promises relate to a well-paid job or a good marriage, the messages are nearly always the same: 'If you do what I say, if you trust me, then your life will be infinitely better—not sometime in the distant future, but today! Right now!' For those who seldom have access to any opportunities at all, such offers are too tempting to pass up. They don't realize that these fraudulent promises come at a terrible price.

Therefore, one of the biggest challenges the anti-slavery sector faces is how easily people accept such promises. Most trafficked persons are simply naïve. They want so much to believe the promised opportunity is real that they put common sense and logic aside.

The factors that allow many trafficking scenarios to occur include two fundamental elements: trust and deception. Human trust is one of the most powerful tools available to traffickers. Many traffickers are people from within a victim's community, who are known to them, and trusted.

It is important to note that many people who are lured and trafficked do not lack intelligence; the traffickers are just very convincing liars.

While working for the UN in Thailand, I once offered a reporter an interview. Because of my schedule, I set up the meeting in a small coffee shop outside the city centre. Within a few minutes, the reporter was talking about how stupid migrants are to allow themselves to be trafficked. She went on with these insensitive statements for several minutes.

Finally, I said to her, 'With all due respect, I have some questions to ask you. First, what do you know about me?

Not much, right? Second, you came to meet me here today at this little café based on faith. You assumed I was a good, respectable guy. Right? But what if I wasn't? What if I was a trafficker? I'd be able to take advantage of you right now. A van could pull up and snatch you. Do you see my point? Do you consider yourself to be stupid? Of course not. But this is often how these things play out. This is how trafficking works—as part of a simple exchange when a person least expects it. It isn't stupidity, it is a misjudgment of trust.'

This woman was completely taken aback by my statements. She began to look around nervously, as if there might be some truth to the notion of me being a trafficker. After I offered this comment, her condescending tone completely changed as we continued the interview. While she didn't apologize for her insensitive comments, she did send a nice follow-up note that thanked me for the briefing and the 'important lessons'.

The following statement from a trafficker I once met in Bangladesh demonstrates the lengths to which these people go to deceive a victim:

> 'Sometimes, we use veteran prostitutes as bait. We hire a man to pretend to be her husband. Then, as a couple, we rent a small house. While living in that house, we become friendly with the community, particularly with the young girls. Then, one day, our prostitute asks one of the girls if she would like to go out with her to a movie or to a park. Most parents do not allow young girls to go out, except to schools. So the woman working with us will lie to the parents. She then takes the girl to the brothel. As soon as she arrives there, she is surrounded, and it is too late for her. Among this crowd there are young boys. They start teasing and touching her until they ultimately rape her as an initiation into the trade. We make sure the village knows

> *about what happened to her. Once spoiled, her community will*
> *not accept her back, and she belongs to us.'*

Of all the factors contributing to modern slavery, the most difficult one is deception. If a person is inclined to trust others, they can easily be tricked and deceived. Since many traffickers are accomplished liars, it is not difficult to persuade a person to go down a wrong path. For me, this represents over three-quarters of the cases I see related to modern slavery.

Debt bondage and credit bondage in trafficking scenarios

Traffickers also enslave and hold victims in place through one of two key mechanisms involving money: debt bondage and credit bondage.

Debt bondage is a situation where advances in cash are paid from the trafficker to the victim, her family, or to others, which the victim must 'work off' as an indentured slave. Whether through force, physical or mental abuse, or some other form of coercion, the victim is maintained at the exploitation site until the debt is satisfactorily paid. Many times, the lender uses false accounting methods or charges excessive interest, sometimes in excess of a thousand per cent. The bonded labourer does not know when the lender will consider the debt paid, so the length of service is undefined and extensive. Such debts provide the exploiter with justification for maintaining his or her victim in bondage.

Credit bondage is a situation where, over time, the trafficker does not pay the victim their wage. The victim remains at the exploitation site in the hope of recouping their earnings and minimizing their losses. This process of waiting can take months or years. Sadly, most employers have no intention of ever paying the employee.

Getting a person into slavery through debt is often very easy. When I lived and worked in Bangladesh, I saw people entering into slavery conditions for less than $10. The scenario might go like this: a family earns no more than $2 per day. They live from hand to mouth, using this limited money to cover their food and housing. One day, a family member becomes very ill. To save their life, the family needs $20 to buy medicine. Since they have no money to offer, they borrow this amount from a money lender who is also involved in human trafficking. But since they will never earn more than $2 per day, they will never be able to pay back both the loan and the interest. To recover their investment, the trafficker will insist that a family member works for a duration of time to pay this debt. With excessive interest, this could take a year or more. This is a common form of human slavery.

Here is an example of how debt bondage is used to hold workers in place:

> *Mr Sharma runs a small battery factory in northern India. The difficult, dangerous work results in a high employee turnover. Mr Sharma resorts to taking on trafficked persons. Realizing that he can obtain far higher profits by forcing people to work longer hours with little or no pay, he continues to demand more and more from his staff. To maintain compliance, he regularly beats and threatens the factory workers. To justify keeping them there, he creates a situation where they fall into a deeper and deeper debt with him. He charges them for housing, food, medical care, and more. Before long, his workers are trapped in a cycle of debt bondage. Since he recruits people from Bangladesh who don't understand the language or the culture, it is much easier to get them to comply with his wishes. As the existing employment regulations are poorly enforced by the state, his illicit business continues to flourish unchecked.*

On a number of occasions, I met people suffering from this kind of debt and reached into my pocket and paid it off. It was never more than $50. For me, it was a simple act of kindness that didn't require much money. But for the person who was trapped in this situation, it meant everything. It just goes on to show the disparity that exists between different classes of society.

In some cases, a trafficker delivers a person to an exploitation site and then receives a cash payment. In essence, victims are sold to the business. For victims to regain their freedom, they are expected to work off the amount of money the business owner paid for their purchase, along with additional fees added to the original amount. An impossible debt holds the person in place.

Compared to many years ago, slave prices have gone down in modern times. The average price for a slave in the mid-1800s was approximately $40,000, as adjusted to current values. Today, depending upon the location, a slave can be acquired for as little as $90, the cost of a pair of running shoes.

Family involvement in modern slavery

Not all traffickers are strangers. Many are known to the victims and may even be members of the family, as in this next example:

Ali is a young man from Bangladesh with dreams of owning his own land. During a business trip to India, he learns that there are people looking for young women to work in brothels. A trafficker tells him that he can earn a tidy sum of money simply by bringing pretty young girls to a certain location. Upon returning home, Ali decides to talk his eighteen-year-old cousin, Sushma, into going with him back to India for a short visit. To avoid trouble with the family, he tells Sushma that he has already received her father's permission to travel with her. Since Sushma lives in a male-dominated society, she accepts his word. They take off for India without anyone else knowing that they have left. Upon arriving, Ali sells the unsuspecting Sushma to a brothel and walks away with a thick wad of cash. Knowing that if Sushma ever returned she would not reveal what really happened to her for fear of being cast out, he is confident his crime would never be exposed.

Many times, I have heard people talk about how, in some impoverished countries, parents are so poor that they will sell their children for money. While this does happen in rare cases, it is the exception, not the rule. Whether they are rich or poor, most parents love their children and want what is best for them. In most cases, if a child is taken away, it is most likely on a false pretence.

Kidnapping

Kidnapping is another tactic that is used by traffickers, but it is much less prevalent than most other approaches. It is much easier to transport a person who is willing rather than using force with people who are not. When people can be deceived into believing that they will benefit from going somewhere, moving them to another place is a much easier task. Compliant victims will help traffickers evade the attention of border police and customs officials. The victims will be unlikely to attempt an escape until it is too late. In contrast, kidnapping victims tend to fight, kick, and scream, which presents obvious risks for traffickers.

Here is a statement made by a trafficker interviewed in a prison in Bangladesh. It contains details of some of the means by which women and children can be kidnapped:

'We collected the children from one of the local schools in Khulna. These schools have a fixed van-puller who picks up and drops off the school children. Sometimes, these children are taken to parks with the school's permission. We contacted one of these guys and asked him to bring a few children to us. We agreed to pay him 60,000 Taka. One day, when the van-puller found suitable conditions to abduct the children, he took them to the Rupsha River. He informed us to meet him at a certain spot to collect them. After collecting them, they were trafficked to India through the Bhomra border. Their parents never knew what happened. We only needed five kids, but he brought seven. We made some extra money that day.'

Tragically, these children were used for carrying highly toxic liquid from big drums to smaller containers. The owner of the factory had adults do the same work but found that the liquid fumes damaged their brains within three months, rendering them incapacitated for life. But for young children, the damage to their brains happened after a longer period of six months, so their youth allowed them to get more work done before they suffered extreme brain damage.

The same trafficker also told the following story:

'We use different techniques and strategies to collect girls. The main things we look for are physical beauty, a young age, and someone who is in a relationship with a boy. Most of the girls we traffic are from middle-income groups. To select our target, we

usually observe girls going to school. After we have watched her
for a few days and have decided to take her, we make our plan.
After lunch, when all the girls returned to school, we would call
her to draw her away from the others. Then we would force
her to get into our car. Most young girls end up in the brothels.'

Traffickers violate many laws and human rights during the process of recruiting, transporting, harbouring, selling, and maintaining the person. Their brutal tactics can include torture, rape, beatings, threats of violence, threats of reprisals against family members, deprivation of food, and physical confinement. Each of these elements contributes to placing and maintaining the person in a slave-like situation.

Confinement, imprisonment, and isolation in trafficking scenarios

These two accounts demonstrate the extent to which traffickers go to hold a person in place:

'After arriving at the factory, one of the first things I was
shown was a short video on a mobile phone of a young man
being beaten to death with a club. When I tried to turn away,
they held my head in place to force me to watch the video till the
end. I still remember all of the blood. There was nothing left of
his head when they were done. I was told that if I ever tried to
run, this would happen to me and my family members. From
that point on, I did everything they said.'

'After the two of us tried to run from the brothel, a group of
goondas found us at the bus station and brought us back. Both
of us were tied up. To teach us a lesson, they took lit cigarettes

and began to burn our private parts. They then took a coke
bottle, covered it with spicy sauce, and thrust it inside me.
I passed out from the pain.'

Using threats to hold a person in place is a very effective approach. If someone said to you, 'Do what I say, or I will hurt your mother and father,' how could you ignore this kind of threat? While it is unclear what percentage of threats are ever acted upon, who would be willing to take this risk?

For many victims, confinement and isolation from others prevent them from seeking help. These factors are often the case for victims of domestic servitude and forced marriage. The tactics used to enforce this isolation often include violence or threats of violence. I heard this story in India:

'I worked from 5:00 a.m. until midnight every day for three
years. I never had a day off, or any time to myself. The compound
door was always locked, and the walls were so high, there was
no way I could have escaped. One day, I heard children playing
in the street. Since I was desperate to leave, I put a note in a
plastic bottle and threw it over the wall. All at once, they went
quiet. For three days, I waited; nothing happened. Then on the
fourth day, a person from the police came. While my employer
tried to say there was no problem, I ran up to the policeman and
begged for help. If I hadn't thrown that note, I would still have
been there today.'

Confinement, imprisonment and isolation serve to control the victim. Trafficked persons are often restricted physically and socially, and their privacy and social support systems are taken away. Within these settings, the victims only have access to other victims or the traffickers and those who are aligned with them.

Corruption in trafficking scenarios

Corruption plays a major part in the trafficking problem. Through bribes, many trafficking scenarios are able to thrive without interference, and many legal cases don't go through as officials are paid to look the other way or drop a case. Corruption can also enable irregular migration by facilitating the passage of victims past border control officers. There would be much less trafficking if the rule of law was more strictly enforced and more proactive legal systems and procedures were present to address this systemic problem. Corruption is not something that can be tackled in a short period of time. Solutions need to be found and tailored within existing local systems. Here is a typical example of corruption related to the trafficking issue:

> 'Whenever the police came to do a raid, we knew about it beforehand. When the team arrived, one of the officers would come to the door. All we needed to do was to hand him an envelope full of money. He would then just turn around, and the problem went away. There is nothing that a wad of money can't buy. Everyone, I mean everyone, has their price.'

This chapter offers an overview of the factors that allow typical trafficking scenarios to take place. Having visited countries all over the world, I have come to realize that these techniques and approaches appear to be universal. I have always been surprised by how much consistency there is related to this criminal endeavor.

PART II

Ending Modern Slavery in our Generation

Chapter 6

Are We Losing the Fight?

Chapters 1 to 5 have focused more on contextualizing modern slavery and presenting a brief history of present-day advocacy work. From this chapter onwards, I will provide concrete examples of how we have moved forward and contributed to the advocacy, implementation, and measurement of impact related to this important cause.

Our collective impact

Why are there still so many people trapped in situations of modern slavery? Why are so few of the victims being rescued? Are the counter-trafficking responders not doing their job? Are they lazy? Are they not working hard enough? No, these are not the reasons. People who work in this field are some of the most committed professionals you'll ever meet. Most, like me, have been severely affected by the victims they have seen and the situations they have observed. We are all super committed. The answer to this question is much more complicated.

With so much tremendous profit, criminals have powerful motivations to protect their businesses. Unlike drug trafficking where a product must be repeatedly moved to earn revenue, in human trafficking, once the victim is acquired, money begins to flow and continues to flow.

One reason that the impact of the responders is minuscule is that human trafficking and slavery issues continue to be variable and confusing to almost everyone dealing with them. Unlike other areas, there is not one single crime to focus on; it is often a collection of dozens of crimes that unfold over extended periods of time. To make sense of them, we package this 'collection of broken laws' under the heading of 'human trafficking or modern slavery'. There are definitions for what trafficking or slavery is and isn't. Figuring out what falls under this category can be so frustrating that the police and the legal systems often don't bother to try.

Another reason for the lack of progress is the number of people who are addressing the problem. While it is estimated that there are over 500,000 criminals, there are only about 20,000 people globally who work full-time to address the problem. With greed as their motivation, many of the traffickers are incentivized to do whatever they can to earn as much as possible off the backs of their victims. They don't have to follow any rules or regulations. From this, it is clear that the counter-trafficking community is simply outgunned.

With so many people suffering, it can no longer be business as usual. We must all come together in this world and take a stand to help them. Governments, the United Nations, NGOs, the private sector, and the general public must all work together to make this happen.

What can be done to increase the number of victims helped? Can this problem really be solved? For me, the answer is a resounding 'yes'. But for this to happen, we have to do things much differently. We must put in place a second-generation model of thinking. We have to shift from relying solely on the limited capabilities of the counter-trafficking community, to asking everyone to play a role. Here are some measures that would help.

More funding

One option often suggested is that we need to significantly increase the amount of funding available to the governments, the UN, and NGOs. But what if, by doubling the available funding, we only double the number of people helped? This would raise the percentage from 0.2 to 0.4 per cent, equating to 200,000 people helped out of 40 million. It still puts the level of impact below 0.5 per cent.

It is important to go deeper into this option. Do we even know whether the governments, the UN, and NGOs are the best or only organizations to help reduce slavery? When it comes to providing support to victims, they are probably best suited for this. But what about their ability to do things that will actually reduce the numbers? In my opinion, many NGOs are better equipped to address mainstream development issues related to healthcare, education, and poverty reduction; but, when it comes to criminal activities or labour issues, many simply don't have the right skills or experience.

Based on this analysis, I'd argue that we need to create a united front that combines the collective actions of all: governments, the UN, non-profit and community-based organizations, the private sector, faith-based groups, schools, universities, and the general public. If funding was used to bring this about, I feel that the outcome would have significantly more impact.

The management of multi-stakeholder efforts is the process by which organizations come together to plan, monitor and improve their relationships amongst themselves. It typically involves analyzing the needs, expectations and aspirations of community members. Multi-stakeholder partnerships help in raising awareness among key partners and their constituencies. They also allow for an entire community to be calibrated to the same set of interventions and outcomes, thus creating a more united front. If implemented in an effective manner, this approach can have a significant impact in increasing implementation outcomes. This topic will be explored in more detail in the coming chapters.

More research and data collection

Because of the clandestine nature of human trafficking, in most countries, there is little standardized information available on trafficking trends such as modes of recruitment and the number of persons trafficked annually, while the information that is available is sometimes incomplete, biased, or unsubstantiated. This has resulted in counter-trafficking programs being set up without a sufficient and accurate understanding of the dynamics and complexity of the problem. Consequently, an intervention might not be responsive to the true situation.

One reason for the scarcity of empirical information on human trafficking is that quantitative research and data collection instruments required to address this criminal activity are yet to be fully developed and tested. For example, research

methodologies that could be used to systematically track
victim cases and criminal behavior are seldom shared within
the counter-trafficking community. Often, information that
is available is not subjected to analysis, and there is therefore
no new input to be applied to potential solutions. Also, the
limited information that has been analyzed is often not
translated into action, resulting in the loss of the information's
potential impact.

To increase the reliability, availability, and the use of
accurate data and analysis, the human trafficking sector needs
a stronger empirical base. This will result in:

- better understanding of the constantly evolving
  trafficking flows and mechanisms,
- identification of what works and does not work, so
  that interventions can be adjusted for maximum
  responsiveness,
- consensus on what needs to be done, how, and by
  whom, and
- the establishment of up-to-standard and
  operationalized policies, mechanisms, service delivery,
  and capacity for responsiveness region-wide.

Examples of existing reports on human trafficking include
the Global Slavery Index and the US State Department's
Annual Trafficking in Persons Report. The information that
they contain allows for in-depth understanding of human
trafficking on a global and regional scale, and can be used
to create legislation and develop tailored solutions in each
country. These reports have also allowed for different types of
human trafficking to be recognized and addressed based on
frequency and severity of cases. However, although they have
many detailed data points, these reports are also subject to

limitations, and more organizations should therefore start to place importance on data collection to increase the information available for use in the fight against human trafficking.

For example, the US State Department's Trafficking in Persons Report is considered by some to be too political, resulting from a portion of the information being skewed or biased because of strained relationships between the USA and a given country. Likewise, some researchers feel that the methodologies used in the Slavery Index are too simplistic and insufficient to calculate accurate modern slavery projections.

The counter-trafficking sector must find a way to collect, analyze, and understand the problem. One idea that has been discussed but not yet put into action is the development of a field-based programme for training researchers and data collectors in new and innovative approaches to identify trafficking. Such a programme could be attached to a university in order to allow teachers and students to work together in a field setting.

A comprehensive plan

Unlike other development sectors, such as HIV/AIDS, child survival, poverty alleviation, and education—those that have a plan of action—the counter-trafficking sector lacks a comprehensive framework from the highest level to the community level. Such a plan is needed to help identify goals, objectives, and activities for each of the stakeholder and responder groups. Such a comprehensive plan would allow groups and organizations to have a better understanding of their role in the overall solution. The 4P framework—prevention, prosecution, protection, and policy—mentioned in Chapter 4 has been used by the counter-trafficking community for over twenty years and is a starting point. However, updates need to be made to take into consideration lessons learned and emerging best practices. For example, there needs to be more emphasis on the role of the private sector and the importance of data collection and use.

When forced labour is included in the counter-trafficking approach, there are other factors that need to be inserted into the paradigm. The counter-trafficking sector needs to make finer distinctions between trafficking outcomes. For example, addressing forced prostitution requires a completely different set of skills, processes, and procedures than forced labour inside a sweatshop or on fishing boats. There also needs to be a nuanced approach to national laws. For example, in some places, like Hong Kong, prostitution is not illegal, but soliciting is, so trafficking data may be affected by the way it is categorized by the law enforcement officers when a crime is reported. Making distinctions between each of these scenarios is necessary to identify viable interventions. There is no one cookie-cutter response to the issue, as it is too diverse and complex.

One of the best examples of a viable framework can be found within the HIV/AIDS sector. Realizing the importance of a blueprint for the future, the global AIDS response community developed a plan that highlighted the need for leadership and teamwork at all levels. The Global Strategy Framework on HIV/AIDS drew upon the lessons from the past to map out a path for the future. Above all, it called upon all sectors of society to show leadership in galvanizing the response to HIV/AIDS—among people of all ages in towns and villages, companies and community organizations, countries and continents.

This plan has helped to engage and empower governments, NGOs, civil society and people living with HIV/AIDS to come together to implement a united, consolidated response. It has brought about a tangible behaviour change within the response community, from a centralized and medicalized HIV response to one that is driven and delivered by communities. This has resulted in HIV/AIDS programmes extending their reach and impact. It has also helped reduce redundancies and costs. Only when all these forces joined in a common effort was the world able to expand the fight against the epidemic to decrease risk, identify vulnerability, and make an impact.

This same process needs to be implemented within the human trafficking sector.

An example of this kind of strategy was launched in October 2020 by my organization, the Mekong Club. Within the white paper titled, 'A United and Strategic Response to Modern Slavery in Global Supply Chains: Eliminating Labour Rights Violations While Maintaining Profitability', there is a ten-year blueprint for how the private sector could address modern slavery within the manufacturing sector.

This blueprint has been well-received by our business community. In order to implement the activities outlined in the document, six organizations have come together to refine and improve the plan of action. A consolidated, unified website is being developed to offer a focal point for bringing the manufacturing community together. Once these elements are in place, a comprehensive outreach effort will be rolled out for recruiting additional partners to expand the implementation. Since the plan describes what activities are required during a specified time period and what resources are needed to be successful, this community action becomes the framework for implementing what has been decided by the community itself. This approach demonstrates the importance of a well-established, well-coordinated framework and a plan that enjoins different stakeholder groups to work towards eliminating human trafficking. To address modern slavery in all sectors, similar strategic plans need to be developed.

More evaluations

Beyond data collection, there needs to be more emphasis on comprehensive, evidence-based evaluations to track progress and determine the success of programmes. While the counter-trafficking sector has been around for over thirty years, information is still lacking on what are the most cost-effective, impactful interventions available to address or reduce the problem. Few comprehensive evaluations have been done. The potential danger of not evaluating the work is that activities could be having no impact or actually be increasing the risk of human trafficking.

For example, in Thailand, one form of intervention that has been used for years for reducing human trafficking is keeping girls in high school for two more years. In the past, many girls would drop out of school after the tenth grade, and a percentage of these girls would become trafficking victims. To prevent this, incentive programmes were put in place to help keep these girls in school until the twelfth grade, based on the assumption that remaining in school would decrease the chances of them becoming victims of trafficking. However, when this programme was later evaluated, there was a notable increase in trafficking. This is because after the girls graduated, their families felt that they were educated enough to get jobs in the capital. But due to the highly competitive job market in the city, most were unable to secure jobs. Too embarrassed to go back home, some of these girls became victims of trafficking. While girls' education is an important tool for development, if these programmes do not include education about the risks of modern slavery, they could result in an increase in trafficking victims.

Likewise, some low-interest loan programmes have been created in Cambodia, Laos and Myanmar which offer poor families an opportunity to set up businesses locally; these were marketed as 'counter-trafficking programmes'. While these efforts have succeeded in allowing small businesses to grow and thrive, when evaluated, the United Nations found that a percentage of the profits generated were invested in migration opportunities that resulted in trafficking. In this case, communities that didn't have a history of migration now had the resources to do so, increasing the number of potential human trafficking cases.

It is essential to better evaluate existing programmes to determine what is effective and worth replication and what needs to be replaced with new programmes.

Packaging of interventions

Many counter-trafficking efforts are done in isolation. Each organization develops a unique approach based on its mission instead of collaborating to create a comprehensive plan. The main reasons for this lack of collaboration are fear that other organizations will get a funding advantage, interagency differences in perspective and approach, and a lack of understanding of the importance of consolidating activities. One of the best ways to increase the efficiency and effectiveness of a counter-human trafficking initiative is to link the efforts of different organizations together through umbrella grants that ensure collaboration is built into the basic design.

For example, to get the most out of a protection response, having a programme that addresses the needs of someone from the point at which they leave the exploitation to the time when they are settled in a stable living situation is critical. In Cambodia, several United Nations offices worked together to set up a network to address the needs of trafficking victims. One NGO was able to offer shelter support to help victims receive healthcare, counselling, food, housing, and an opportunity to decompress. Another NGO offered travel support back to their home community. These interventions helped victims transition back into their normal lives. Another NGO provided regular follow-up care to identify the trafficked person's long-term needs, offering victims a stable support system. Another organization provided job training and job placement. Through this united approach, victims were able to navigate their lives after being trafficked. Had these services not been linked, many victims would have been vulnerable to being re-trafficked.

The same situation should be considered for organizations that offer a legal response. Instead of working independently, if a consortium of organizations were brought together under a single umbrella, the outcome would be more impactful. For example, when working on prosecution cases, the following skill sets could be brought together: proactive investigation, legal training, legal follow-up, victim protection, and legal reform. Many trafficking cases fall apart because the raid and rescue are not tied to a long-term prosecution strategy, or the victim protection needs are not planned before the intervention.

Finally, the same can be said about preventive activities. If the prevention community was brought together to identify common, standardized messages that were reinforced in many different ways, a better outcome could be reached. For example, when I was working in Bangladesh, we hired a communications organization to collect, analyze and consolidate all of the counter-trafficking prevention messaging available. The range of different messages was found to be haphazard and lacking in any validation. Once this process was completed, we presented the results to the counter-trafficking community. Based on this effort, feedback was collected to develop one consistent messaging approach that could be used by all. This approached allowed for all of the prevention efforts, including awareness raising, training, posters, and public service announcements to be done in unison, in a way that communicated the same message across all facets of society. This helped increase message retention and the desired behaviour changes we had been seeking to help prevent human trafficking.

By packing together individual initiatives, a more efficient and effective outcome can be achieved.

Private sector involvement

Another approach often suggested is to encourage the private sector to become active in the fight against human trafficking and modern slavery. In the past, there has been little incentive for companies to bring them to care about this issue. In fact, it has been considered too sensitive and something to be quietly avoided. This is due, in part, to investigative journalistic and activist efforts that aggressively 'name and shame' companies to get them to make changes in the way they run their businesses.

What can the private sector do? They can start by looking closely at their business to determine if there are any risk factors. For example, within manufacturing supply chains, factories sometimes restrict workers' movement, hold their official documentation to prevent them from leaving, force workers to do overtime without pay, or hold them in place with fraudulent debt. Using a range of tools, companies can take specific measures to maintain a slave-free supply chain by conducting investigative audits that illuminate the real conditions faced by workers. They can also offer training to staff and suppliers, as well as put in place systems and procedures that reduce the chances of collaborating with companies that exploit people in modern slavery.

The Mekong Club's experience working with the private sector has demonstrated that with only a small investment, victims of forced labour can be identified and helped without having to raise NGO, UN, or government resources. In fact, compared with traditional interventions, the return on investment can be more than five to one. We have identified and implemented initiatives that can be targeted in the following sectors:

Manufacturing: With extensive supply chain and manufacturing channels in multiple, usually underdeveloped countries, it can be difficult for companies to monitor their many supply chain outlets. Increased understanding of the ways that slavery can appear in supply chains is vital to effecting change. Issues of interest include developing risk assessment tools, standardizing auditing methods and approaches, consolidating information collected from audits across industries, and improving communication within companies across internal divisions.

Financial services: Annual profits from modern slavery are estimated to be $150 billion, most of which goes through the global banking system. Being on the frontline of financial transactions, the financial services industry has a distinct advantage in being able to identify suspicious activity by traffickers and stopping it. Issues of interest include the importance of using big data to help identify 'red flags', understanding criminal patterns to develop systems to track their activity, and the importance of training to develop the capacity of employees at all levels to find potential problems.

Hospitality: There are dozens of touchpoints where modern slavery can occur in the hospitality industry—staff recruitment and food sourcing are only two examples. Due to the vast size of the industry, eradicating this issue has the potential to affect thousands of lives. Issues of interest include how to train staff at different levels to detect the problem, how to address the four potential vulnerabilities within the hotel industry—forced prostitution, forced labour within supply chains, third-party service contracts, and construction—and how to develop standardized responses across hotel chains.

Retailers: Any amount of product sold that is found to have a link with modern slavery or child labour puts a retailer in a position of liability and potential reputation risk. Urged by public pressure and the need to safeguard their businesses, many of the biggest retailers worldwide have engaged in more proactive monitoring activities. Issues of interest include understanding how to inform and educate suppliers, how to identify the boundaries of the supply chain involvement, and how to respond to a reputation crisis.

To create a united front on the issue, companies can facilitate multi-stakeholder initiatives that join the private sector, workers, labourers, civil societies, and governments. It is possible for the private sector to identify and root out bad businesses when the right resources are allocated for it. The necessary skills and capabilities to tackle the problem, whether it be legal, compliance, accounting, communications, or financial expertise, exist within the sector. What is needed is for the private sector to be brought into the discussion in a respectful way that considers them a part of the solution, not the problem. Doing this will significantly help reduce the number of human trafficking victims.

The impact of COVID-19 on modern slavery

Since January 2020, the COVID-19 outbreak has been affecting the entire world. To slow the spread of this virus, many countries have implemented extreme quarantine measures that have significantly affected a full range of businesses. With factory shutdowns, order cancellations, workforce reductions, and sudden changes to supply chain structures, many workers have lost their jobs or have been furloughed for an extended period of time. As a direct result of this unfolding situation, the risk of modern slavery has skyrocketed globally as the dire economic impact of this pandemic has increased.

For example, Asian garment workers supplying global fashion brands lost up to $5.8 billion in wages between March and May 2020, as the COVID-19 pandemic led to store closures and cancelled orders from the West. Many unemployed workers were forced to turn to exploitative jobs, and some even made their children take up work in order to survive. As one Bangladesh worker stated, 'With no options, I went to a local factory and told them I'd work for no pay if they gave me food and a place to stay. It was either this, or living on the street. This was a matter of life or death for me.'

According to a study that came out in September 2020 by the analytics company Verisk Maplecroft, falling jobs and orders will affect up to 60 million people who work in Asia's garment industry alone. This is just one sector. Many of those who have lost their jobs are unable to find work with comparable wages and benefits. One worker said, 'I go to my old factory every morning. They tell me to come back tomorrow. But it is always the same. They say the orders have not come and we don't have any work for anyone. It has been months now. We are down to one meal a day. I don't know what to do next. I'm desperate.'

Human traffickers prey on those who are economically vulnerable. Without a paycheck, and generally unable to rely on personal savings, the possibility that an unemployed worker will find themselves bearing excessive debt significantly increases. This debt might come from local money lenders, community institutions, or family members. In taking on debts that they cannot repay, workers leave themselves open to exploitation by these various parties. Employers may offer to lend money to their employees, and in some cases this might be the only solution. However, it could also lead to a debt bondage situation where the worker falls under the control of their employer due to the debts incurred. The situation is generally worse for migrant workers because many of them already have debts incurred as part of the recruitment process. One worker stated, 'I have been out of work for three months. I have had to borrow money from my neighbours. When they were no longer able to help, I had to turn to local money lenders. Now these people are coming around asking me to pay them back. With no job and no money, I have been told that my son will be taken away to work. They said if I don't agree, something bad will happen. These are dangerous people. What can I do?'

As this situation continues to unfold, more and more women and girls are also being forced into prostitution to earn money for food and to cover the bills. One woman in this predicament said, 'I had no choice. I had to begin selling myself. It was either this or we wouldn't eat. I would have done anything else if I could have. But there is no work. Nothing.'

The pandemic has changed everything. As a result of the global economic disruptions, the World Bank estimates that up to 500 million people might slip back into poverty. This will completely erase twenty years of progress made in raising families up.

To bring about a change, we must first do everything we can to understand the true situation on the ground among vulnerable communities. Armed with this information, we must find ways to help get these people back to work. This might require job training and job placement programmes.

You and I

While the organizations from the relevant sectors have a crucial role to play in fighting modern slavery, there is still one other group that is just as, if not even more, important: you and I. I'm convinced that by working together, ordinary people from all over the world can spearhead a wave of good that can help us achieve a slave-free world.

In fact, we have a historical precedent for this. One hundred and eighty years ago, there was a global abolitionist movement. At that time, people debated whether slavery should exist. Eventually, those who fought to end it prevailed.

What if we generated this same spirit today? What if everyone who thought about the exploitation of enslaved people felt compelled to take action? Couldn't we achieve a similar breakthrough? While 40 million people in slavery may seem a large number, compared to the 7.8 billion people who share this Earth, it is actually quite small. We must start a new abolitionist movement.

Why will this work? Because human beings have an incredible ability to solve problems when they put their minds to it. Consider the immense sophistication of our social structures. Our massive, functioning cities address the needs of nearly every citizen, offering access to food, shelter, transport, jobs, leisure options, and more. Our science and technology can solve huge problems, fight diseases, entertain us, and educate us. Our legal systems provide rule of law, justice, and fairness in our world. Our education systems teach, inspire, and motivate us to grow. The list of human accomplishments goes on and on.

On an individual level, we all have unique skills and abilities that can be applied to combat human slavery. A student, a banker, a business owner, a homemaker, a farmer… everyone can help. This, I am convinced, is the most important thing we can do to end slavery—to educate, inspire, and get the world to step up in a united way.

Why has this approach not taken hold before now? The chapter that follows will discuss this fundamental question in detail. For me, it is one of the most important questions of our time.

Modern slavery isn't someone else's problem. It belongs to us all. We have to take care of our own. These people are desperate. They need our help. If we don't do this, millions will suffer. There are times in life when we must all step up. This is one of those times.

As Margaret Mead, a famous American cultural anthropologist, once said, 'Never doubt that a small group of thoughtful citizens can change the world; indeed, it's the only thing that ever has.'

Chapter 7

Heroes

While the previous chapter focused on the activities and initiatives of organizations that have been set up to address the counter-trafficking issue, this chapter will shine a light on each of us. It will make a case for the importance of individual initiatives in the fight against this terrible crime against humanity.

Everyday heroes

What the counter-trafficking world needs are heroes—everyday heroes.

Most of us feel that heroes are people who demonstrate impossible feats of bravery and courage to help those in need. While this is one example, not all heroes exist in comic books or movies. They are not just people who risk their own lives to save the helpless but also ordinary men and women who give of their best selves for others.

I consider everyone who steps up to help our world, no matter how big or small the gesture, to be a hero. This spirit, some would say a divine spark within us, can be recognized and nurtured to reach its full potential. Our world could be a much better place if more of us accepted this reality and owned it. This is one of the essential messages I hope to convey in this book.

Taking this concept further, a heroic act can be represented through a person who does something quite simple and seemingly insignificant. I see this nature in someone who takes the time to help an elderly person cross a busy intersection, a teacher who helps a struggling student with a new concept that just doesn't make sense to them, a police officer who helps a victim of a crime to feel secure after just having been violated, a mother who helps her son when he scrapes his knee, or the person who smiles at someone who is having a bad day.

You can also be a hero by taking the time to learn about something and helping personally. It doesn't mean that you have to give up your life and go to Cambodia to fight slavery. It could be a simple monetary gift to a struggling NGO, volunteering at a local shelter, or the important act of getting the word out to others.

In all these cases, it's not about the size of the gesture, but rather the gesture itself—**the selfless act of kindness for another without any expectation of something in return.** The gesture can be as subtle as reaching out with your hand to offer a reassurance of love. What is the main ingredient of this act? Doing something for people who are in need. Why should you do it? Because it's the right thing to do. Because they simply can't help themselves. Your humanitarian instincts can lead to extraordinary caring.

There is a hero within each of us. It is the voice of good, of righteousness, of action, and of love. In this modern world, this voice often receives very little nurturing. It lies dormant much of the time. As a result, a great latent force of regular, continuous good never reaches its full potential. This heroic part of ourselves is capable of waking us up to the issue of modern slavery, and inspiring us to help. The question is, how do we tap into it and make it into a force for good? If 10 million people contributed some time and effort, these gestures would add up to something huge. This is my simple life message.

Heroism is that part of our mind that whispers into our thoughts, urging us forward, to step up, to act, to get involved, and to do the right thing. There are times when this voice is silent and other times when it is so clear, it is as if someone is shouting at us. Our inner voice helps us see the path ahead, often persisting until we listen and respond. We can try to ignore it, but if we do, we often feel regret. It is the voice of goodness. We want to help. We want to be involved. We want to have a sense of purpose. When this voice becomes inescapable, we want to surrender.

But despite this force, many people do not heed the call. Over the years, getting people to the point of surrender has been a challenge. While I know there are people who care about modern slavery, there appears to be a counter-voice that talks them out of it. This voice whispers, 'You are too busy to help. You have nothing to offer. The issue is too big to tackle. It could be dangerous. What if you don't like this work?' Understanding that our minds can work against us when it comes to making a commitment to help is part of the solution to move forward.

Velleity

During a passionate presentation I did in Malaysia, my
frustration over the lack of public involvement came out in a
short rant at the end of my talk. A person from the audience
came up to me and said, 'Your presentation was all about
velleity.' When my facial expression revealed that I didn't
understand what this person was talking about, he went on to
define the word for me. Velleity means 'a wish or inclination
not strong enough to lead to action'. He said what I described
was something the world has faced from the beginning of
time. He went on to state that 'people are great at observing
and yearning, but terrible at following through.'

In one of my TEDx Talks, I presented another example of
velleity. I said, 'Let me explain—there is this line. (I hold my
arm upright.) On one side of the line, a person learns about
an issue, then comes to understand it, then begins to care, and
then gets right up to this line. (I slap my arm to demonstrate
that the line has been reached.) The moment we cross this
line into action, we are doing something for others or for the
world—we are part of the solution. You are a hero. But to
get over this line can be one of the most difficult things a
person can do. Why is this important? Because this is a line
that can change the world. Even the smallest gesture and act
can be helpful—an act of kindness or a simple task on behalf
of another. It all adds up. But as simple as it is, for many, the
journey never reaches its full completion.'

Addressing a crisis

The clearest example of the impact of this heroic voice
can be found when we are confronted with a crisis. When
we come upon a traffic accident, most of us instinctively stop

and offer help. Within an instant, we know what needs to be done, and we act. We don't have to be taught this—it's part of our core being. Some of us may have had an experience like this one:

> '*I watched as the car in front of me ran off the road and hit the pole. Something told me that I needed to act. I heard the voice in my head. It walked me through what I needed to know. It was as if I was already programmed to act.*'

This situation happened to me when I was eighteen years old. After seeing the accident unfold, I pulled over and approached the car to check for casualties. I found the driver to be awake, but he was trapped in the car. There didn't appear to be any life-threatening injuries. Since this happened before cell phones, I flagged down a car and asked them to find a phone and call 911, the emergency call centre. I stayed with the person who was trapped within the car and made sure he was talking and remained conscious. Ten minutes later, an ambulance arrived. I stayed to report what I had seen to the police and then went home. This whole process seemed so natural to me.

If a person is struggling to hoist their bag into the overhead compartment on a plane, we automatically step forward and help. What needs to be done is so clear, there is no questioning it. In fact, if we choose not to do something, that inner voice becomes louder and louder. Inaction is not an option. Many of us have a genetic response mechanism within our DNA. This is our inner heroic voice.

Our personal motivations to help

Sometimes, those who have suffered in life are more inclined to act heroically than others. People who have been exposed to poverty, oppression, and violence understand what it is like to be in need. Their life experiences sensitize them to those who require help. When I provided disaster relief as a US government official working in Sri Lanka immediately after the 2004 tsunami, some of the most dedicated people who stepped forward were those who had experienced the greatest loss. They recalled the pain and despair they had experienced. Some of them mentioned that they got involved in other causes because they felt a need to repay the kindness that had been shown to them. There is something significant about having gone through a tough period that motivates a person to help others through their own pain.

Of the volunteers I have had the honour to work with in the counter-trafficking sector in Hong Kong, at least half seemed to have experienced some major trauma in their life at one time or another. This theme was so prevalent in my work, that we once set up a conference to help offer personal healing.

Sometimes the motivation to volunteer is based on a personal recovery; other times the person has never really got over the pain they absorbed. But something compels them to help others—as if by doing so, it will lessen their own pain.

Devoting oneself to a cause in the service of others

Some heroic efforts result from a chance event that requires immediate action—pulling a child out of a burning car, saving a drowning person, or stopping a violent act. These events require a death-defying, split-second response. This is what many of us think of when we define a hero.

But there is another form of heroism: the long game, when someone chooses to devote their life to the service of others. In the counter-trafficking world, we see this among service providers who work in shelters, legal offices, counselling centres, and vocational training offices. This is heroism in a different form. Unlike the hero who gains the limelight for an instant response, many of these long-term heroic efforts go unnoticed. But, nonetheless, they are equally valid. The following statement offers an example:

> '*I have done raids and rescues within the brothels for over fourteen years. This work can be very dangerous. The people we are going after can be cruel and vindictive. I do this work because I care about the people who need our help. I sometimes feel I do it because I don't see others coming forward. When I stop and try to think of something else I could do instead, I can't come up with anything else. This is who I am and what I do.*'

Our kind deeds have a way of generating more kindness. We should all try to take any opportunity to carry out heroic acts on a daily basis. The gratefulness that comes along with these actions can motivate others to follow.

Spontaneous acts of kindness

One afternoon, as I was walking down a busy street in Hong Kong, I saw an old woman pushing a cart full of used cardboard. As she crossed the street, her load fell off. Within seconds, people came from all directions to help her. First there was one, then two, then five. Several of these good Samaritans helped reload the cart. Others directed traffic away from the group. The group worked together as a team to ensure that the load and the woman made it safely to the side of the road.

But this kindness did not end there. One of the bystanders pushed the cart to its final destination. Each of these acts of kindness was small, but combined, they added up to something quite extraordinary. The goodwill that played out enriched each actor in this small drama. The wave of kindness couldn't be stopped. They became a heroic mob.

I have two recurrent questions related to this:

- How do we tap into such generalized goodwill and use it to help stop modern slavery?
- How do we generate this same interest in helping the men, women, and children suffering in these conditions?

Clearly the potential is there. It just needs to be harnessed.

If we were to ask the average person how they would like to be remembered, many would say, 'I would like to be considered kind, generous, and helpful.' One comment made by a fifth grader sums this up well: 'I feel good when I help my neighbour. He is old and needs someone to help him do things. It makes me feel so good inside. It feels good to be good.'

Part of the reason why this doesn't happen more often comes down to how people interact with the world these days. Each morning, I take the train to work. For every 100 people I see, I'd estimate that probably ninety-seven of them are staring at the screen of their phone. This is how many of us collect information about our world. Across that screen, there might be news stories about earthquakes, violence, slavery, wars, hunger, poverty, politics, and the like. We observe this information, perhaps note it, but then we move quickly on to the next topic. Life can become an endless stream of data related to all things.

The problem with this approach is that we seldom take time to stop and engage on issues because we are so consumed in watching the live stream pass by. We have become, to a great extent, a world of observers rather than doers.

Ironically, I found it easier to involve people in activism work in years past when information on the topic was sparse and intermittent. While we waited for new information, we had to talk about what we did know, debate it, and process ideas in our minds. Once we worked things out, we could move forward with a plan. This happens less nowadays.

Goodness within

Most of us have enough generosity of spirit to change the world. Yes, there are bad apples, but goodwill always triumphs. We need to develop and foster the good in ourselves and encourage the good in those around us. This process is based on our collective sense of compassion. Our compassion demonstrates that we care about others, treat them with kindness, and feel a strong desire to help people in need. In this way, compassion is a miracle of 'empathy combined with action'.

Children often express this naturally with a hug, hand-holding, or by saying something kind to help someone who appears to be sad or upset. But we all have this tendency. If you are walking down the street and the person in front of you trips and falls, you'd help them up. There is no thought involved in this process; it's an automatic response.

Open the doors of one person's compassion, and we discover that it is contagious. The doors of large efforts toward human improvement often swing on small hinges.

The problem is that many of us tend to restrict this automatic tendency to a limited number of circumstances. What we should do is find ways to open up this natural inclination. Ordinary people can expand their better instincts to address societal issues that are important but not directly relevant to their own lives.

A hero understands that almost all people respond to goodness, that individuals and individual actions matter, and that regularly showing examples of people being good to each other will inspire similar actions in others.

For some, doing good is an intention that is ever present; it aligns with a person's hopes, dreams, and aspirations. Achieving good helps them to fulfil a sense of purpose that aligns with who they are as a person. *I feel I am a good person. I have always felt this way. When I can help, it reinforces this part of myself. I want to be good. I want to be helpful. It is part of my purpose in life. I am so blessed to have this nature.*

This chapter highlighted that everyone who steps up and helps another, no matter how big or small the gesture, is being heroic. In today's world, this voice too often lies dormant and receives very little nurturing. This innate heroism can be used to help combat and eliminate human trafficking. It just needs to be channeled and directed in the right direction. The approach for achieving this outcome will be discussed later in this book.

Chapter 8

Lessons From the Field

The next six chapters will focus on learning from experience. This will help educate and inform human trafficking managers, frontline workers or anyone else who wants to learn. The text will outline the lessons learned from my own experiences, the experiences of others, the impact of projects and programmes, and life concepts.

Both good and bad experiences are equally important and represent valuable assets we can use. Once acquired, we should always look for ways of passing on the wisdom gained from our experiences. During my nearly four-decade-long career, I have been blessed with great mentors. When these enlightened people shared stories about their own experiences, they often taught me valuable lessons. What sometimes surprised me was how some of the stories initially didn't seem relevant to my needs. But later in my life they did, and they helped me to grow as a person.

When I offer advice to my colleagues who are working in the field of human trafficking and modern slavery, I often share the following simple truths:

- First, most of what we do to address human slavery involves working with others; at times, there's a potential for drama, conflicts, and intrigue;
- second, logic, common sense, and practicality are not always the key to success;
- third, what we see is not always what we get; we must see beyond what appears to be obvious;
- fourth, we should accept our mistakes with goodwill and a positive mindset, and use these experiences to process and improve ourselves; and
- fifth, if we go through life with a spirit of accepting the unexpected, we will seldom be surprised or feel let down.

Understanding these truths will nurture the hero inside of us. I hope that through my experiences, you can gain some wisdom and insight to help you in your own journey.

Note that not all of the stories address the issue of modern slavery. So why are they included? Because many experiences can teach us lessons that can be applied to other aspects of our life. For example, a story that addresses the education sector can be applied to the human rights sector. This is because so much of our life experience is based on encounters with human nature in one way, shape, or form.

Many of these experiences changed my behaviour, my attitudes, and my approaches to life, most often for the better. We can all learn from each other. We all have similar lessons. We should all be open to changes that can allow us to reach our full potential. I offer these stories as my gift to you.

Below are a sample of lessons I learned from my field experiences living and working in Asia. They will offer some insight into the complexity of issues that are often faced by people who are working on the frontlines.

Moral and ethical dilemmas

There was a time in my career when I was actively involved as an advisor in supporting groups that conducted periodic raids and rescues within the Mumbai brothels. I would receive a call about a brothel that had a half-dozen underage girls who had been trafficked from Nepal. After receiving this update, a raid would move forward. A group of police and NGO workers would be recruited, the raid would take place, and the girls would be taken to a shelter for their protection and rehabilitation. Several of us received death threats regularly as a result of our involvement.

During one of these calls, I came to realize that they were doing an operation on the same brothel that had been raided twice before. When I asked about this, I was told that the past raids had taken place, but the authorities had been unable to shut down the business. Because the owner was well-connected with corrupt police and local officials, he reluctantly forfeited the girls, but remained in business. Within a week, he had procured more girls, and he was up and running again with even more exploited victims.

After getting off the phone, I stopped and thought about this situation. By pulling the girls out without closing him down, we were actually contributing to a situation where more girls were being trafficked. We were inadvertently increasing the number of victims. Having come to this conclusion, I called the NGO and asked if they should do the raid. I explained that if we continued down this path, more and more victims would be trafficked.

While I don't know what eventually happened with that brothel, during the time I was involved in providing advice for these raids and rescues, this business remained open. This means that the girls who had been recruited were not saved from this terrible outcome. Throughout my career, I have sometimes had to make tough choices. The solution to this problem came down to the math. Unless the brothel was being closed for good, it did not make sense to do the raid. We would be contributing to the trafficking problem, not solving it at the root issue. This meant that the girls who were there would have to remain enslaved to avoid more from following. This was a moral issue that weighed heavily on my conscience.

During my public health days, we had to make similar choices. There was once a time when we set up a successful acute respiratory infection response programme that saved up to 10,000 children a year. How did we know this? Because the data clearly reflected this achievement. After running it for several years, another donor approached us and asked if they could adopt it. This group had taken over several of our programmes in the past, and some of them had been abruptly discontinued. Understanding this reality, we resisted, but then finally agreed after some significant pressure from the government. Two years after this deal, the donor forfeited their commitment, and the child mortality figures went up again. While another donor eventually picked up the programme, it took over eighteen months to be finalized. In the meantime, thousands of children unnecessarily died as a result of this situation and the decision we made years before. To this day, I still feel guilty and haunted by it.

Lesson: Decisions that are made related to human trafficking and public health can have a significant impact on the people we serve. Some of these decisions have moral and ethical implications that must be taken into consideration. Sometimes the best of two bad alternatives must be selected.

One of those very sad moments

In different parts of the world, strict cultural norms govern what happens to girls within a traditional society. I saw this reality in the worst way following a trafficking case in Bangladesh. It involved a fifteen-year-old girl whom a local trafficker kidnapped and took across the border to India. Once there, the trafficker immediately sold the teenager to a brothel. While most girls in this situation are trapped for several years, a police raid rescued this young lady after only three weeks. By then, the girl had been forced to have sex with several dozen men. For a young, unmarried Muslim woman, few fates could have been worse. Her society considered her spoiled.

As part of the raid, a newspaper team covered the event. Despite their professed ethical code against revealing victims' identities, the article included the names of those rescued and where they came from. This information somehow made it back to the survivor's home community in Bangladesh. Within days, everyone knew her tragic story.

Following the raid, the girl spent three weeks in an Indian shelter where she received counselling, medical care, food, and love. After that, social workers brought her back to Bangladesh where she waited an additional two days at a local shelter. I was invited to accompany the young lady back to her home village. I agreed, in the hope that I would gain a better understanding of how the repatriation and reunification process worked.

Two hours after leaving Dhaka, the capital city, we arrived at her village. Because so few people would visit this location with an official-looking vehicle, word spread like wildfire before we even exited the car.

As we rounded the path into her family's compound, in front of the house stood her entire family: her father, mother, an older brother, and two younger sisters. On our side stood an NGO representative, the young girl, and myself.

For several moments, everyone just watched each other. When the daughter started to move forward with her hands stretched outwards, the father put his hand up and said, 'Stop.'

She halted. I could see and feel that the entire family had love for her. I sensed that they wanted to run up and scoop her into their arms. Instead, a horribly different outcome unfolded.

'You have to go,' said the father. 'You can't stay here any more.'

The young girl remained in place, not knowing what to say or do. She knew what was happening, but she chose not to believe it. 'It is me, father. I am home.'

'You can't stay here. We know what happened to you. You will have to leave.'

'But I didn't do anything, father!' she cried out. 'I was just walking down the road when I was kidnapped! I didn't do anything!'

'I am sorry. What happened to you can't be changed. You have brought shame to our family. You will have to leave. Now, go!'

'But father, I didn't....' she started to say before he cut her off again.

'Just leave,' he demanded as he held back his own tears. 'We have your brother and sisters to think of. We need to ensure they have a chance to get married someday. Your shame will prevent that from happening. Now go!' He turned to walk into the house.

When the mother started to walk towards her daughter, the father said to his wife, 'Come inside now!'

This was one of those times in my life when my heart completely broke. Despite their tremendous love for this girl, sadly, their sense of societal obligation overruled that love.

We brought the girl back to Dhaka. She got a job in a garment factory, but several months later, she disappeared. No one knew what happened to her. I sometimes wonder if she died from a broken heart.

Lesson: We must understand the importance of societal norms and practices. They can supersede a family's love for their son or daughter. Over time, we can only hope that these traditions will change. The unfortunate victims of sex trafficking in such societies require specially designed care and support. Another important lesson from this anecdote is related to the role the media plays in contributing to the outcome. While the media is supposed to respect the confidentiality and autonomy of victims, in many countries, this often doesn't happen. In their drive to offer a titillating story, a victim's right to privacy can be completely disregarded. One of the positive outcomes of this tragedy was that it convinced us to put in place a comprehensive programme to train journalists on how to write an ethical article that respects the rights of victims.

Less is more; simple is good

Over the years, I have helped set up many development programmes across Asia. These experiences taught me that we must not put all our faith in our own expectations of the final outcome. This lesson played out time and time again during my stay in Bangladesh.

For example, to help educate communities on the dangers of human trafficking, a partner agency developed a comprehensive safe migration curriculum. It represented a full day of material focusing on everything the UN offers related to safe travelling practices for migrants.

Before taking the training, a pre-test was offered to participants. But something shocking happened after a post-test was given at the end of the training. Many scores remained the same or actually went down. The training provided so much information that it overwhelmed and confused the participants. The excessive details caused them to lose their perspective and their sense of priority.

Following this disappointing outcome, a team of consultants was asked to assess what could be done to reverse this situation. Over a two-week period, they used focus groups and small group discussions to identify the simplest way to prevent human trafficking. What they discovered was amazing in its simplicity. It was a stroke of genius.

Instead of a long, drawn-out training, the villagers were taught to do only ONE thing: 'If a person wants to take your son or daughter away to India to get a great job, don't say no, say yes. But also say that a family member will go along to India.' It was then explained to them, 'If the deal is good, the recruiting agent won't care, and the process will move forward. But if the agent terminates the arrangement, it is probably a trafficking situation.'

Six months after providing this advice, we returned to this community. The villagers were very excited. They said about 60 per cent of the time that they offered to send a family member along with the recruiting agent, the deal fell through.

They said they now understood that this would have turned out badly.

In many parts of the world, children are told not to take candy from strangers and not to get into cars with them. This is a universal message regularly reinforced and accepted by everyone. Because this village had experienced this prevention outcome first-hand, it too became a similar kind of message— one that would be repeated countless times by everyone in the village.

Lesson: We must understand that often, less is more. A simple message directly related to a problem offers protection that is clear, understandable, and effective.

Off to the hills

During my early counter-trafficking years in Nepal, there was a girl named Heena who had just returned from the brothels in India. She had been trafficked when she was only fourteen into one of the most notorious sex establishments in Delhi. She spent three gruelling years there before being rescued by an NGO team based in India's capital. During our interview, she talked about the terrible rapes, torture, and abuse she endured daily. She suffered from a range of sexually transmitted diseases, including AIDS. It was one of the most terrible stories I had heard.

After six weeks in one of the local shelters, her anger continued to grow. On a number of occasions, she vowed to the shelter staff that she would travel into the northern villages, which had produced many victims, in order to share her story. She said she was determined to prevent any more Nepalese girls from ever experiencing the same terrible ordeal she had endured.

Several counsellors tried to talk Heena out of her decision. They warned that a young girl shouldn't be travelling alone in the dangerous hills of Nepal. They cautioned that her health would worsen without regular treatment at the shelter. Undeterred by these statements, it was clear that nothing was going to get in her way. Realizing that we couldn't change her mind, we asked if she'd agree to travel with a companion. After much persuasion, she finally allowed a male social worker to accompany her.

Over a six-month period, Heena traveled throughout Nepal, telling her story. In each village, she'd locate the centre square, often under what they called a People's Tree, where she'd sit down and begin recounting her story. At first, there would be five or six people listening. Then others joined, until the crowd swelled to up to a hundred people. At the end, many of the villagers appeared shocked and horrified by her emotional testimony. Others cried when they heard the fate of so many young girls from their own country.

At the end of each talk, someone would inevitably raise their hand and say, 'What can we do to protect our community? What can we do to protect our young girls?' At this point, the social worker would stand up and say, 'I am glad you asked that question. Down the road, at another village, we talked about this and came up with a plan to start a neighbourhood watch. At the village before that, they decided to put in place a school registration system.'

The nice part about this approach was that solutions were identified on the spot. Many suggestions could be put in place with little or no effort. The community's participation in the process ensured that the suggestions remained relevant to their own cultural and traditional needs. The collective discussion also helped in raising awareness.

Lesson: It is important to support programmes that are developed and managed by local communities. Their involvement in the process ensures more ownership and long-term sustainability. Such programmes can be put in place with limited resources. Heena's courage helped prevent others from experiencing her fate. She continued her travels until she grew too sick to go on. With no medication at that time to treat AIDS, I was told that Heena eventually died. This was the fate of most of the girls I met back then.

Holding a hand

As a public health officer, I managed a range of programmes throughout Nepal. Most of them focused on mainstream development issues, including reproductive health and child survival, but I sometimes found myself exposed to other, more uncomfortable ailments.

During one of many field trips, a fellow health worker asked if I'd like to visit a leprosy colony. The thought of this visit intrigued me professionally, but I found myself thinking of the leprosy scenes in the epic movie *Ben Hur*. This Hollywood blockbuster included a disturbing depiction of this disease that had a devastating impact on me as a young boy. People with this disease lived in dark, smelly caves to hide their shame.

As we walked down the path to this isolated community, several elderly people came forward to greet us. They were clearly thrilled to see my guide. While I had come across many health conditions in Nepal, it was very disconcerting to see people missing fingers and toes, as well as sores across their arms and legs.

Without hesitation, my guide reached out to each friend, taking them by the hands. Holding them closely was a loving gesture of acceptance. She then turned and introduced me to the assembled group.

While the reality was that this disease was not highly contagious and there was virtually no chance of infection, my struggle was based on misplaced emotions, not logic and common sense. As I stood there facing feelings of dread, the old woman standing before me was waiting to see what I would do.

While everything within me wanted not to engage, as I looked into her eyes I felt her pain, her need for acceptance, and her need for understanding and compassion. With clumsy hesitation, I reached out and shook each of her hands. I then went down the line and shook everyone's hands. Beneath my fingers, I could feel their coarse, dry stubs.

While I was glad I did the right thing, I also felt ashamed I hadn't immediately put their needs ahead of my own. I was not at risk, yet I indulged my own insecurities.

Lesson: We can find inner strength to deal with uncomfortable situations. Courage is made up of the mental or moral strength to venture, persevere, and withstand danger, fear, or difficulty. We often speak of it but too seldom act.

Reaffirming our commitment

Now and then, something happens that reminds us of why our work is so important. One day, one of my staff came into my office and said that there was a man downstairs who came to the United Nations building to meet me. I asked who it was. My assistant told me that he was some villager from Myanmar. Because I was busy, I asked if one of our other staff could meet with him. I didn't have the time or the interest.

Twenty minutes later, my assistant returned, stating, 'He said he will not meet with anyone else but you, and he will not leave until he does so.' Curious by this definitive statement, I reluctantly agreed.

When Aung entered my office, I could see he was a man with a purpose. He was small and thin with a set of facial expressions that left nothing to the imagination. He had several prominent scars across his face, as if he had been in an accident, or through a terrible beating. Even before I was able to say something to him, he began telling me his story in broken English:

Three years ago, I was in Myanmar in my village. At the time, the government troops were regularly attacking our communities. Not knowing what might happen, I was married. She was a village girl whom I had known all my life. I loved her deeply.

My wife and I had two weeks together before the violence came to our village. To save our lives, we ran into the jungle without anything but our clothes on our back. After three days of walking, we managed to get to the Thailand border. Realizing that we hadn't had anything to eat for days, a nice man came to us and offered some food. After eating, we told him our story. He seemed kind and compassionate.

He described that he could get me across the border. He went on to state that he had a van that was going from Chang Rai, a northern district, to Bangkok. He said we could ride in the van to the big city and then easily get a job there. He repeatedly said this would be the answer to our dreams and offer safety from the government troops. Knowing that there were many Burmese people working in Thailand, we were most grateful.

After crossing the river at night, we were shuffled to a small van with eight other people. No one said anything. The men who were in the van seemed very angry and aggressive. They were not like the kind person who had helped us back in our country.

Three hours after leaving, the van stopped abruptly, and the door swung open. Two men grabbed my wife and started taking her away. When I tried to intervene, one of the men said, 'You took a ride in this van. This costs money. You don't have any. Your wife will have to work off this debt.'

The more I tried to stop them from taking her away, the more they fought back. Before long, I had three men beating me. I passed out.

When I woke up, I was on a fishing boat. I was in the middle of the ocean. One of the other sailors, a Burmese man, came to my bedside and explained what had happened. To cover my own debt, I had been sold to the captain. He told me not to give them any trouble. If I did, I would be hurt.

Desperate to find my beloved, I got up and told the captain I had to get back to Thailand to find my wife. He didn't listen. The more I pushed, the more they beat me. At one point, I was beaten so badly that I nearly died.

Realizing that I couldn't help my wife if I was dead, I finally began to comply. But EVERY waking moment was consumed with one thought. I needed to find my wife. It was my fault she had been taken. I agreed to the arrangement. I needed to find her. I loved her.

Three years passed before I could escape. Our boat was anchored near an island. One night I managed to jump off and make it to shore. That was four months ago. Somehow, I managed to get to Bangkok. After going to the police, no one could help me. I have tried everything. Then someone from an NGO said to go to the UN. That is why I'm here. I need to find my wife. I did this to her. She is my life and my love. I MUST find her.

You have to help me. You have to help me. You have to help me.

He grabbed my hands, and I watched as tears streamed down his face. His sheer anguish was unrelenting. His desperation to find his wife went right down to his soul. His entire body shook from his frustration.

I felt his pain. I imagined what I would have done in the same situation. I realized I'd do exactly what he did. We fight for our own.

While I agreed to do what I could to help, I knew what had happened. The traffickers had taken his wife to some rural brothel. She was gone. Finding her would be nearly impossible. And even if we did, some women in this situation would not want to reunite with their spouse. The shame she felt might be too overwhelming to face.

While I agreed to try to find her, which I followed through with my staff, as expected, there was no sign of her anywhere. While he had promised to check in with me again, he never did.

Lesson: As we do this work, we have to sometimes be reminded of the importance of our efforts. Like anything else, it is easy to go through the motions. We can lose that spark that motivated us in the first place. Events like this bring our priorities to the surface. They help us to re-experience the pain. This can give us a jolt of remembrance.

The criminal element

The real experts in human trafficking are not people like me but rather the victims and the criminals. These people have experienced the process first-hand. Only they truly understand what happens because they have lived it. While we have countless stories from victims, there is a lot less information available from the perpetrator's perspective—they have little incentive to provide these details. Therefore, we often lack an understanding of how a criminal's mind works.

During my stay in Bangladesh, some of my partners received permission to interview traffickers in prison. At first, the inmates repeatedly asserted their innocence. They said they had been falsely accused and should not be in jail.

With little success, we regrouped and considered another tactic. Realizing that many criminals were narcissistic by nature, we remarked to one of the traffickers that many of the prisoners appeared more successful than he. The prisoner's pride kicked in. He argued that he was smarter and cleverer than the other traffickers. Before long, he offered a detailed account of his crimes and schemes. His stories and others like them provided valuable new insights into the criminal world.

As a parent, my heart breaks when I hear a victim's tragic story. It is impossible not to feel empathy and compassion for these hurting people. But the emotion I feel when I hear a trafficker speak is something much different. They inspire fear—fear that these heartless people are out there in the world, willing to do harmful and unspeakable things. Some of their stories are so shocking, you can't comprehend how someone could have such a complete lack of humanity. They speak about their victims as if they are disposable commodities.

One person told me how he would do anything necessary to break the will of his victims. He described this process as if he were taming a wild pony. I asked him if he ever felt any remorse. He looked back at me, not understanding the question. He then said, 'Why should I? It is their own fault. They got what they deserved.'

One hardened criminal repeatedly said, 'They are just girls. They are not worth anything anyway. Who cares what happens to them?' Another trafficker indicated that he was offering a public service: 'If I didn't do this work, men would go around and rape good girls. We need prostitutes to stop this from happening. I should be thanked for the work I do. I make the world a safer place for your daughters.'

But there is another side to the criminal perspective. Many of the madams I have met over the years were once victims themselves. They were trafficked at a young age and forced into the business. Like most victims, they suffered within a cruel exploitative system that demanded absolute obedience. Over time, with few options to escape this world, instead of turning away from it, they learned to embrace it. With each step up the hierarchy, their life got a little easier. Eventually, the brothel owners took notice of their talents and taught these victims to become perpetrators themselves.

Some might argue that these victims/perpetrators had the choice not to follow this path. While that is true, it is not difficult to understand their motives. We all seek a better life. In their thinking, this was the only way to achieve that goal.

Some people ask, 'How could they go from being mistreated as victims to mistreating others? Wouldn't they feel empathy for the new victims who came into the brothels?'

I am not altogether sure why they don't, but this is not a new phenomenon. We see molested children go on to become pedophiles themselves. Instead of appropriately handling the pain they felt, they use it as an excuse to act out. This process happens often to people who are severely traumatized.

Our hearts ache for victims, but the moment they cross over to being part of the trafficking infrastructure, our views on them change. We offer little empathy or understanding for perpetrators. But criminals also need help to become something better than their present existence.

Years ago, I was in Hanoi, and I received a call at my hotel. A local Vietnamese man asked if I was Matthew Friedman. I said yes. He then asked if he could meet with me. As a UN official, I used to get these kinds of calls now and then. It was usually someone who wanted to better understand the work I did and how the UN was addressing the problem.

The next day, we met in a small café. He was well-dressed and well-educated. In fact, I'd go as far as saying that he was very interesting and pleasant.

For an hour, I sat and talked about my work. When I finished, I turned to the man and asked, 'So, what do you do?'

Without hesitation, he said, 'I'm a human trafficker.' As you can imagine, I was shocked. He went on to state that he always wanted to talk to someone like me and thanked me for my time.

While part of me wanted to stand up and storm off, I decided instead to continue talking to him. For the next hour, he described how he trafficked women and girls into forced prostitution and sometimes men into forced labour. I was surprised at how open he was. He didn't seem to hold anything back.

At one point, he handed me his card and said, 'Go ahead and try to catch me if you can. You'll never be able to. I'm too insulated.'

He began by saying my work was a joke. He said, as a criminal, he had the ability to change his approach every day if necessary, to keep ahead of the game. He said that in my world, we followed static plans and inflexible procedures. He was right.

Because we had to abide by rules, he said that we'd never win the fight. He said that in his world, they had no rules. They could be unethical, unconventional, unorthodox, and ruthless. That would always offer them an unfair advantage. He said this was the reason why crime paid. The legal system was too encumbered by processes and procedures that constantly tripped it up. He stated that the criminals always knew what we were doing because we put it out there on our websites for the whole world to see. He said this was like making the battle plans of a military force available to its enemies. He repeatedly laughed about this.

He added that the NGOs and the UN were not equipped to do counter-trafficking work. He asserted that they didn't understand the criminal world. Without this comprehension, they could do little to affect his business. He cited the number of conferences and workshops that NGOs put on to talk about things they did not understand.

Finally, he said that greed was always a much more efficient motivator than the desire to save the world. In his case, the outcome of his work was a handful of cash. It was tangible and real and offered instant gratification. In my case, the profit was 'a person gets helped.' Properly helping a person is anything but quick or easy.

As we were leaving, I said to him that if he ever wanted an honest job, I'd be happy to hire him. While I was half joking, I realized that his knowledge and expertise would go a long way in our fight against the problem. He laughed and said he'd think it over. 'Maybe when I'm old I'll take you up on this.' It was a very surreal moment in my career—one that I will never forget.

Lesson: It is important to learn about human trafficking from those who know it best—the victims and the criminals. Getting first-hand accounts from criminals helps us understand the systems and procedures used to recruit, initiate, and hold a person in a trafficking situation. This is never easy, but it must be incorporated into the work we do.

Feeling bad only helps if we do something about it

The nature of this work causes activists to become exposed to heartbreaking realities. We see or hear of girls as young as five being repeatedly used by pedophiles for sex, teenage girls gang raped by up to ten men at a time, or men who have had their throats punctured with a knife on a fishing boat before being tossed into the ocean to die. Add to this the day-to-day torment and desperation that accompanies these crimes, and you have a perfect recipe for burnout.

Let's face it—most people are simply not emotionally equipped to process these atrocious crimes against humanity. This isn't because they are not professional enough, but because the experiences are so extreme.

I once went to see a counter-trafficking worker in his hotel room and found him hiding in the corner, passed out from having consumed a bottle of scotch. It was his way of coping with the pain. This happens.

A few years ago, one of my staff who ran a hotline out of our office got a call from a young Burmese girl who had been kidnapped. Somehow she had kept her cell phone. As her captors drove her through Thailand, she'd make short calls every time they stopped to use the toilet. While she knew she was in Thailand, she had no idea where. She didn't understand the language and couldn't read the signs.

My staff member did all he could to console the girl and get the details we needed to locate her. With each call, it felt as if we were getting closer to a breakthrough. Then, as quickly as the calls started, they stopped. This event devastated several of my staff. Unfortunately, this kind of result often comes with the work.

The stark reality of the human trafficking situation is that it is very sad and depressing much of the time. Many people who work in this area are seriously affected by their experiences. It is easy to drown in despair. Those who can't overcome this will burn out or fail to be effective. Feeling is important. It motivates and acts as a driving force, but it must be tamed and controlled. Some people can do this; others cannot.

What keeps people like us going? Knowing that there will be more calls. And knowing that next time we might be able to help. It is all about persisting in hope.

Having said this, over the years, I have come to realize that I have my limits. Many times I have been completely shut down by an experience. I am not a superman who can turn everything off and keep forging ahead. Not for long anyway. I will be forever haunted by memories of terrible things I have seen.

Lesson: We must do our best to face the issue, often putting our feelings aside while we do the work. We must be honest with ourselves. If the work is too much for us, we must admit this and let others get on with it.

Helping heroes to see their superpower

In November 2018, I traveled to Washington, D.C., to attend the American Bankers Association's Financial Crimes Enforcement Conference. As a counter-trafficking expert, I was invited to participate in two panel discussions focusing on the issue of modern slavery and the banking sector. Following the second session, one of the bankers came up to me and told the following story.

Three years earlier, he had been travelling with his family across several states in America by car to meet up with relatives. After a long drive, he pulled into a small motel off the highway. Because it had been a long journey, his wife and two teenage daughters felt tired. That evening he went out to get some food for the family. As he was coming back to the motel, he noticed this very young teenage girl being pulled into a room with an older man. He said he remembered she had such a sad, frightened expression across her face. He knew immediately what was about to happen—she was about to be used by this patron. Since he had daughters of his own around the same age, he felt he needed to do something to help.

After dropping off the food, he went to the motel manager and told her what he saw. He then returned to his room, not knowing if anything would happen. Twenty minutes later, there was a police car parked in front of the room. Ten minutes after that, he saw someone being taken out in handcuffs. The young girl was escorted to another car and driven away.

He said he remembered this event because he felt so good that he was able to help this young girl out of this terrible situation. In fact, he went on to say that this was a major milestone in his life—something he felt very proud of.

After hearing his story, I asked him what he did for a living. He said he was a compliance officer focusing on anti-money laundering for one of the major American banks. I asked him if they did work related to the issue of modern slavery. He said they were just getting started in this area, and that was why he came to the session. He went on to say that he felt his job was not very exciting and he wasn't sure how much difference it was making.

Throughout the world, many people in banking compliance do their jobs, not realizing that the outcome of their work could have a major, positive impact on our society. Over the past two years, human trafficking continues to emerge as an important issue within the banking sector. With an estimated $150 billion generated from this illicit crime annually, banks must ensure that none of this illegal money makes it into their business. If it does, and regulators find out about it, the bank can be fined for money laundering.

Many banks are stepping up their efforts to track this crime. This includes training their employees, breaking down crimes into component parts to identify potential links with banking procedures, using 'red-flag indicators' to search their data for nefarious activities, and, if found, sending this information to financial regulators.

With this in mind, I told the ABA banker in front of me that while his day-to-day efforts might not seem as dramatic as his motel encounter, there were many people who could be assisted through his work in the coming years. I went on to say that those involved are our future heroes because what they are doing will help to protect not only their bank but also many other people like that teenage girl. His face brightened. I was surprised that he hadn't understood this before.

I have told this story to many bankers. What amazes me is that many of these people don't make the connection between the important work they do and the enormous value it adds in potentially helping people out of exploitation. For some, this simple story offers an epiphany.

Lesson: Banks and other private sector companies need to understand that by addressing the issue of human trafficking, they are not only protecting their business, they are also helping to address one of the biggest injustices of our time. The outcome will be that many people are freed from bondage. This makes their efforts truly heroic. Helping people to understand that they are heroic can be inspiring. It is a great way to help a community understand their true value. Following a banking event in Singapore, one of the participants said to me, 'I felt really good after hearing the story about how an ordinary banker can make a difference. I thought my job was meaningless. Now I realize it isn't. I am really grateful for this insight.'

Chapter takeaway

Many of the lessons outlined in this chapter are based on the work I have done in the field. They reflect the complexity and diversity of the issues faced while dealing with cultural, traditional and community topics. These anecdotes and stories were offered to help those who might be interested in doing anti-slavery work and applying them to their own efforts. This, I feel, will allow the reader to learn from real-life scenarios and help them be more effective in their future endeavors. Learning from experience teaches us much about how the world works. Here is the good news: to be effective in our work or our personal lives, we don't have to experience everything ourselves—we can learn a great deal from the lessons that others have learned.

Chapter 9

Lessons From Management and Administration

My oldest son, Brandon, is in medical school. Every Sunday, we have a call to catch up. During these discussions, he often describes some of the interesting cases he has seen in the hospital. From these talks, I have come to understand the importance of the concept of 'practicing medicine'. To be an effective doctor, a person has to see thousands of patients. Since each situation is different, this process helps the physician to accumulate the experience needed to understand how to effectively diagnose illnesses. This learning process is continuous.

I feel the same about being a manager or an administrator. This work doesn't just come to us; we have to experience it and learn from our successes and failures. Once again, the learning process is continuous. Issues often faced in this setting might include being understaffed, staffed with the wrong people, facing a lack of communication, poor teamwork, pressure to perform, absence of structure, and the like. In this chapter, I'll describe some of the management and administrative situations I've faced as a means of conveying some lessons learned.

Humble, humble, humble

When I was twenty-eight years old, I worked for an organization that evaluated US-funded international development health contractors around the world. While my job was to collect information for evaluation assignments, before long, I was being invited to participate in some of these events. I went from serving as a support person to being an active member of the evaluation team. I often entered a country, reviewed the operational plan, and made determinations about the impact of the work being done. Over a two-year period, I travelled to more than twenty countries.

The red carpet was rolled out for me, and I was often treated like a king. The thing is, when you evaluate a major development project, your decisions can determine the fate of a multi-million-dollar programme. A company's future can sometimes hang in the balance. For this reason, those being evaluated went out of their way to please the evaluators. That was the way things were.

Being young and inexperienced, I allowed this fawning to go to my head. The more evaluations I carried out, the more full of myself I became. At the same time, I learned how to manage the system to easily get the assignments I wanted. My arrogance was off the chart. I believed myself to be a golden boy destined to climb to the top. There was no restraining my unbridled ambition. When I became a contender for a major promotion, I realized that I needed some long-term, in-country field experience to remain competitive. Accordingly, I took a twenty-four-month fellowship in Nepal.

Within six months, I came to realize that despite what I had originally thought, I was a terrible evaluator. It wasn't that I didn't know how to collect the information, analyze it, and then write up an acceptable report. That part was easy. The problem was that, as an evaluator, I'd fly in and out of a country without spending enough time to understand the nuances and complexity of the process required to implement a project in a field setting. I had failed to comprehend the internal and external politics, the endless administrative delays, the interagency power struggles, the interference by the government, and the logistical issues. It is impossible to understand the extent of these factors until you are faced with them in a real-life situation.

While I was supposed to be in Nepal for two years, I was so humbled by the experience that I stayed there for eight. During this time, I did all I could to gain a deeper understanding of the cross-cultural development setting.

Lesson: It is important for young people to understand that we often leave university believing that we have all the answers. We sometimes view those who are senior to us as being slow and simple-minded. This comes from allowing logic and common sense, instead of experience, to become our guide. In this case, the best thing that can happen is a situation where our arrogance and inexperience can be revealed. Understanding the importance of humility is one of the most valuable lessons any of us can learn.

Honouring the local context

During my early years in Nepal, we spent a lot of time trying to understand a plethora of community development problems. We collected data, analyzed it, and reviewed what activities worked and didn't. Based on this process, we would create an implementation plan. Once the Americans in our office vetted it, I'd take the plan to the Nepalese government and try to move it through their system.

During my first two years in Nepal, I had a terrible track record with the Nepalese government. With each failed proposal, I went back and reviewed my materials. I always came away convinced of the absolute soundness of my rationale and reasoning. I simply couldn't comprehend what I was doing wrong.

At one of our office meetings, I confessed my discouragement to our Nepalese professional staff. I walked them through the meticulous materials I had prepared, and I explained the methodology of my thinking. I repeatedly asked, 'Why can't the government see the logic behind this?'

My Nepalese staff listened with sympathy, but they said nothing in response. Their lack of feedback hurt my feelings. Two days later, one of them asked if I could meet him for drinks after work. I agreed. When I arrived at the restaurant, I saw that three other staff members had joined us. I was really surprised. I couldn't understand what was happening.

Within a few minutes, the mystery unfolded. The senior-most Nepalese put his hand on my arm and said, 'We are sorry about your issues with moving the programme forward. We know how much work you put into it. We also understand the logic you have put forth. It is impressive. But the one thing you haven't learned about this country yet is that logic and common sense are not always the yardstick used to decide whether a programme should move forward. In fact, these factors are less important than many others.'

I looked into their eyes. I could tell that they had sympathy and compassion for me. I could really feel it. They were there to help.

'Listen, Matt. You're an American. We have all worked for the US government for a long time. We admire and respect your people. The four of us are Nepalese. We have lived and worked in this culture all our lives. Like your country, our country has its own characteristics. You value logic and common sense. We understand this and share your commitment to this approach. But in Nepal, these factors are among many. Hierarchies, political will, lineage, customs, and traditions—all factor into our decisions. For you, our reasoning may seem haphazard and cumbersome. But for us, it's just the way it is. If you continue to follow the path you have taken, you will continue to get shot down.'

There was a pause as they stopped to gauge my reaction. I honestly didn't know what to say. Finally, I blurted out, 'So, what are you trying to tell me?'

'We would like to provide some advice,' he continued. 'From now on, if you want to move something through the government, please consider coming to us first.'

I looked back at them, feeling confused. I said, 'I always come to you with my project ideas.'

'Yes, you do,' he responded. 'But you might want to come to us even before you begin the planning process. We can help you decide whether or not the end point is possible. After that, you need to trust us to help you through the rest of the process.'

'What do you mean?' I asked, bewildered. I wasn't sure what they were trying to say. I also began feeling insecure.

'Let's work together on the outcome. Once we agree, let us do our job. Let us be the ones to move it through the system. The American way is to go from A to B; to walk a straight path in the least number of steps. That may work in the US, but it doesn't work here. In Nepal, to get from A to B, sometimes you have to go to C, back to A, off to T, down to Z, and then you arrive. There is an order and a priority to every step. It is impossible for me to explain the way it is. It is just something I know, being a Nepalese person. There are foreigners who speak perfect Nepalese who will also never understand it. It is beyond your comprehension.'

'So, what are the kinds of things you'll do?' I asked, feeling a bit dejected.

'We'll meet with people, sometimes eat with them, or simply visit them at their home,' he responded. 'Don't worry, we will not do anything like a bribe or anything else that is unethical. We will just follow a particular order of things.'

'Okay, so I understand what you're saying,' I responded, finally getting over myself. 'You're saying that as Nepalese people, you know how to get things done. Why don't you ever talk about this in our meetings? This makes sense to me.'

'You Americans don't always listen to what the local people say. You have your ideas and your ways of doing things.'

I had to admit the truth of what he was telling me. Although the agency prided itself on saying that the Foreign Service Nationals were equal with the Americans, this was never really the case. Many of us understood this.

From that day on, I took their advice and allowed them to move the programme efforts forward without my direct involvement. Almost immediately, things changed.

Programme approvals moved forward at a record pace, many obstacles were removed, and our staff seemed much happier. I was too.

Throughout my career, this advice continued to be useful. I have always tried to allow my local offices and staff in different countries to take the lead. When I bestow this responsibility upon them, it usually results in a much better outcome.

Lesson: It is important to understand that our local counterparts are the real experts. They understand the cultural context, the content, and how to make things happen. Investing in them is an investment in success. It doesn't matter who accomplishes the tasks. It's all about getting the job done.

Honesty at its best

At an evening reception in Nepal, I was surprised to run into someone I met years before in Africa. As it turned out, she had followed her husband to his new posting in Nepal. After catching up with our lives, she mentioned that she was looking for a job. She had excellent medical credentials, and I helped her find a position evaluating medical outreach programmes. She eagerly accepted the assignment.

A week after starting her job, I received a late-night call from this woman. She was upset having discovered a very dangerous medical practice of reusing unsterilized needles at a health post.

She knew she must report her finding immediately but was worried that doing so would ruin her chances of working in the country. We both knew that whistleblowers were often ostracized. With the offending organization being so prominent, the fallout could have a devastating impact on its funding. She felt certain this would destroy her career.

We talked matters through, and she chose to hold on to her professional integrity and report the incident.

Despite her concern of a backlash, the opposite happened. Word of her honesty spread. Before long, many sought her services. Rarely had I seen such brilliant vindication of remaining true to one's principles.

A slightly less dramatic version of this lesson had once played out in my life. An agency I worked with had spent millions of dollars to support a major clinical program. On the surface, it seemed highly successful. It supported hundreds of private clinics across a poverty-stricken country. To verify the efficacy of this programme, we commissioned a major study.

When the study results arrived, we felt dismayed. While the facilities provided quality care to the middle class, they failed to help the poor.

When I read the report, I initially thought the information would be buried. Why? If we acted on the report's recommendations, the massive programme would have to be significantly changed. Something previously seen as a major success would be deemed a failure. I had encountered similar situations before, thanks to a pervasive bureaucratic mentality: 'Don't try to fix something that everyone thinks is not broken, even if it is.'

This time, however, something very different happened. When my boss asked me what I thought about the report, I said it was pretty damning. He agreed. I asked him what he was going to do. To my surprise, he took several of us to see the programme's director. Within five minutes, my boss laid out the case that our programme had failed and should be completely overhauled.

Many emotions surfaced in me that day. I felt shocked and surprised at my boss's honesty and candor. I felt absolute pride in him. Instead of hiding behind the programme's reputation, my boss did the right thing. He faced the reality. That moment has stayed with me—one where I saw the right thing to do being played out before me. His decision caused a myriad of changes and headaches. But it was the price that had to be paid to reach the poor, disenfranchised people who needed affordable healthcare.

Lesson: It is essential to acknowledge the importance of our professional honesty and integrity, especially when it involves the health and well-being of others. Our integrity determines our destiny.

Facing problems head-on

In Nepal, I supervised a social marketing company that had internal financial and staffing problems. The donor I represented had many concerns, and I brought in a consultant to offer suggestions. The consultant's report was critical, hard hitting, and recommended major restructuring, including some significant downsizing. If the recommendations were accepted, the organization would have to make painful changes.

While decisions were being made within my office, a copy of the report somehow leaked to the NGO, to the consternation of the staff. Since I brought in the consultant, I became a major target of their wrath. Accusations flew concerning my honesty, competence, and ability to make decisions. The entire process became very personal.

Realizing that whatever was going to happen was beyond my control, I went to my supervisor, took a half day off, and went directly to the organization. I asked the general manager to pull the staff together in one room, where I said, 'I want to begin by thanking you all for being here. I know that there is a lot of talk about the reorganization moving forward. There are many misunderstandings, so I'm here to discuss these with you face-to-face. I'm here on my own time. What is it you'd like to say to me?'

For several long minutes, the room was silent. No one spoke. Finally, one hand went up. It was a question about the transition team that would be brought in and what would be done. After answering this question, soon another followed and then another. For three hours, there was shouting, debating, moments of silence, crying, and finally, it ended. I was able to clarify things that had been misunderstood, provide missing information, and apologize for any mistakes I had made.

I realized that some of my decisions had been naïve or misinformed. I had been in over my head. I saw this and asked my supervisor for help. This humbling experience taught me about my own limitations.

Lesson: What could have evolved into major dissension between two organizations was resolved through constructive discussion. Such common situations can prevent development programmes from moving forward. It's good to take on an issue directly. It's important to clarify what is inaccurate and accept responsibility for our mistakes. This establishes respect and clarity.

Working with what you have

For development workers to do their job in a country situation, getting to project sites is essential. To do this, reliable vehicles are needed. During my stay in Nepal, my organization had a policy that forbade us from buying Japanese vehicles for our partners. We were allowed to buy only American cars. The Nepalese government had to endorse these purchases but did not want the vehicles. There were few maintenance facilities in the country for American cars, parts were impossible to find, and they had such a high gear ratio that many vehicles ended up going off steep roads because they were simply too fast. Many of our programmes were unable to carry out proper monitoring and evaluation because the staff lacked the vehicles they needed to get around.

While we explored our options, nothing proved practical or affordable. Finally, one of our staff came up with a crazy idea—why not bring some old vehicles back to life?

At each district health centre, there were four or five abandoned vehicles parked in the back. Most had been junked because a simple part was broken. With no maintenance budget to buy new parts, these vehicles were left to rot. Some of them needed parts that cost very little money. When we realized the number of potential vehicles that fell into this category, we checked our internal policy and found that we could spend unlimited budgetary funds on vehicle repair. The plan fell into place.

We went to the Ministry of Health and offered them a proposition: if we agreed to rehabilitate the vehicles, would they allow us to use them for two years? By the end of this time, we'd hand them over in pristine shape. Because the vehicles were such eyesores and demonstrated an inefficiency of the government, they agreed to let us take a bunch of these vehicles and use them.

This programme became a great success. We solved a problem that once seemed unsolvable in an efficient and cost-effective way. After two years, we offered to hand them back to the government. Having received new ones from other donors, they declined and said we could keep them. This gave us a constant supply of vehicles for a fraction of the price of new ones.

  Lesson: We must find ways to use what we have available to us. Innovation and ingenuity offer cost-effective and efficient solutions to most problems.

Fast-tracking the legal system

In my early years in Nepal, one of our biggest issues was corruption. A sex trafficking case would be filed at the district level, the criminal would be questioned, but within hours, a bribe would be paid and the criminal, released. This predictable outcome discouraged victims from presenting their case. Given that this corruption was endemic and ingrained in the system, clearly it was impossible to fix it in the short run.

  A local group came up with an ingenious approach. They identified a few police, prosecutors, and judges who were honest and sympathetic to human trafficking issues and began working with them. Once these honest people were identified, others came from referrals within their own networks. To gain their support, the NGO shared detailed stories about the victims they sheltered and their many issues within the legal system. These simple procedures significantly helped reduce corruption.

  In Nepal, a human trafficking case must be filed within the district where the crime took place. To allow this new system to work, an NGO representative would travel with a victim to the local police station to file a case. Moments later, a call would be made to a sympathetic prosecutor in the capital, who called the district station and asked that the case be transferred to Kathmandu. This reduced the chances that a bribe could be paid at the district level before the case made it to the courts.

Once the accused perpetrator arrived in Kathmandu, the case was fast-tracked and given high priority. This approach worked well because it avoided corruption almost altogether by identifying and empowering the portion of the system that actually worked. As one lawyer stated, 'We created a "fast track" within the overall legal system that helped us navigate and bypass corruption from within the system.' Very quickly, the number of cases reaching a conviction increased from less than a dozen to several hundred.

Lesson: It is important to find solutions from within existing systems. Each and every bureaucracy has positive loopholes that can be used to keep the legal system going. Finding them can be a challenge. But once identified, amazing outcomes can follow.

Is this really me?

Working at the United Nations, I witnessed a good deal of interpersonal politics. All bureaucracies face this kind of issue. It goes with the territory.

At a major international conference, I attended the evening reception. Not knowing anyone there, I strolled up to several people I had chatted with during breakfast. Over coffee, we exchanged superficial comments about the weather and our food options. What happened next surprised me. These four individuals were in the middle of a conversation about me. Obviously, they didn't know I was their subject. The talk was hearsay because none of them had met me before.

'He is trying to take over the human trafficking sector singlehandedly,' said one person. 'He wants to build an empire.'

'I heard he turned the Vietnam delegation against the Thai delegation,' said another. 'He must really be out of control.'

As the conversation continued, the content grew more outrageous. Apparently, I was notorious. I didn't know what to think. Part of me wanted to walk away, but I was so intrigued that I simply stood and listened.

As the stories unfolded, I began to grow angry. What they were saying was not true. Deep down inside, I felt a voice gaining strength. I should take a stand and challenge this attack on my character and integrity. As I was about to explode, another voice came forth. Its simple message: 'Try to understand.'

Finally, I spoke. I hardly knew what would come from my mouth. 'Excuse me for interrupting, but I need to confess something. My name is Matt Friedman—the one you are talking about. I'm sorry I didn't say something sooner, but I guess I was intrigued to hear how infamous I am. I am surprised to learn I'm such a larger-than-life figure.' I laughed.

For a time, there was silence. Clearly, they felt embarrassed and mortified. The two voices inside me competed for dominance: do I explode, or do I laugh it off?

I reached out my hand, smiled, and said, 'Hi, my name is Matthew Friedman. If you have time, I'd like to talk with you all and get to know you.'

What followed was amazing. Each of them shook my hand, and we had a wonderful talk that lasted nearly an hour. We talked about how rumours get started, how things like this had happened to them, and how slandering a colleague was often an accepted distraction that created division and reduced our potential to work together. We also clarified some of the statements about me and I explained my view on the issues. Our mutual insights proved invaluable to all of us. I am far from perfect. Some of their impressions might have been caused by me, so this helped me to change some things.

Let's face it, human beings have a tendency to gossip. Gossip is usually based on limited information passed from person to person. This results in distortions and misinformation. As we talk about others, it is safe to assume that others talk about us. We should not take it personally. We should use every opportunity to engage with others who may have a negative impression. We all have good and bad elements, but gossip offers little in the way of a fair perspective. Wherever possible, correct misperceptions of yourself.

Lesson: We don't have time to let such distractions hold us back. We must find ways to walk a positive path. Engage those people who don't care for us with goodwill and an openness to learn.

The enemy within

Over the years, I have faced numerous different trafficking situations, many of which involved people trapped in seemingly hopeless circumstances. While I dealt with a great deal of frustration associated with criminals, often the biggest problems were with others working in the counter-trafficking sector, along with our respective bureaucracies.

One such case was related to a major project within a UN agency that was beginning to do well. Before long, donors took notice and started offering additional funding. With limited resources available, competing agencies saw this successful programme as a threat that steered potential funding sources away from them. Instead of celebrating the success of this group's work and focusing on improving their own performance, the other agencies took aim at the project. Soon, whatever collaboration had existed among these entities was replaced with back-room attacks and power plays. Over time, the project suffered so much damage that it lost its effectiveness. Something good passed away forever. The traffickers won this round.

On another occasion, an NGO reached out to others in a spirit of collaboration. They set up a meeting to bring the community together. Feeling that this effort should be made by another organization, a rival NGO set up a separate meeting a few days earlier. Within a short time, the community began to take sides. Instead of working together, the result was division. The traffickers won another round.

Another time, an NGO running a shelter negotiated a partnership with organizations that carried out raids and rescues in a neighbouring country. The rescue organizations started sending more and more victims to this one shelter. Cooperation was replaced by resentment and jealousy. The other shelters circulated rumours of human rights abuses, damaging the thriving NGO's reputation. The accusations proved to be false but ultimately damaged donor confidence in the NGO and the counter-trafficking effort in general. The traffickers won another round.

Collaboration is a basic concept that we in the counter-trafficking world often discuss, but less often achieve. We know that far too often, collaboration is lacking. Competition and turf issues prevent us from fully cooperating. To avoid this outcome, collaboration must be intentionally built upon a foundation of trust, mutual respect, and a united purpose. When people accomplish something within a collaborative effort, they usually step up to take joint ownership of the results. Ownership means we tend to remain committed to solving the problem. This is the road to assuring a positive, supportive initiative.

Lesson: We must understand the importance of collaboration. Imagine how much more we could accomplish with a unified approach. Imagine how effective we could be as a force of one, a force of solidarity. What stops us? We should emphasize what is most important—the whole community helping those in need. We work not for ourselves or our organization, but for people who need our help.

True feelings

As a manager, I sometimes had to make choices that my staff didn't like. These decisions were based on funding levels, programme priorities, donor expectations, etc. While I hoped never to offend or disappoint, this was sometimes an unavoidable outcome. As a result, there were times when some staff members resented me for decisions they did not like.

During a management assessment, one of my country offices was asked to do an internal review. After two weeks, a thirty-page report outlined activities and future priorities. After sending it to me, I reviewed the report and made a dozen or so comments, none of which were major—they had done a great job.

After reading my comments, some people were obviously not happy. In response, they circulated the report among themselves with comments meant to poke fun at the process and me. As the staff members added to the text, the comments became increasingly mean and disrespectful. Of course, this version was not meant for my eyes.

Unfortunately, one of the staff accidentally sent this unofficial draft instead of the formal, sanitized version to me.

I read the text and realized my staff's true feelings were there for me to see. Wow!

I read the comments several times, then left for a short time to consider what had been said. I felt anger, resentment, and an intense desire for revenge. I had no idea what to say or do.

I called a staff meeting two days later. After some small talk to set the stage, I handed out copies of the report. I asked them to turn to page five, where they realized I had their 'internal' version of the report. Their faces revealed sheer horror.

Though I initially wanted to blast them, I confessed that at times I had written similar comments about bosses. I even offered examples. I told them I understood they had issues with me and asked if we could discuss each problem in detail. What might have been a bloodbath turned into a conversation that healed wounds, offered clarity, and fostered forgiveness.

As these things happen, we can either become bitter and hardened, or we can learn to be better human beings. In my case, I have always strived to improve. So let me be clear— while some of my stories may seem a bit idealistic, they come from many good and bad experiences that challenged how I thought and acted.

Lesson: When we allow true feelings to be expressed, we can work together to achieve the highest possible outcome. What is the biggest lesson learned here? A positive approach always trumps a negative approach. It opens doors and fixes things. This is a truth that I came to understand over time.

Chapter Takeaway

It is important that I say something for the record. Over the years, I have made many mistakes as a manager. I have allowed pride, jealousy, resentment, anger, and more to cloud my decisions. At times, I've had favourites. I have engaged in politics and power plays that sometimes failed and sometimes succeeded. I have hurt people and been hurt myself.

But over time, I have learned from these experiences. I have tried my best to be a manager who is honest, decisive, empathetic, compassionate, supportive, focused and creative. I do this by not just managing but also by practicing and learning from what I do and how I do it. By shedding light on this reality, I hope others can benefit from my own experiences.

Chapter 10

Learning from Mistakes

Let's face it, we can all learn how to live a better life from our own mistakes and the mistakes of others. As Eleanor Roosevelt, the wife of president Franklin D. Roosevelt once said, 'Learn from the mistakes of others. You can't live long enough to make them all yourself.' This topic is so relevant to our lives that Goodreads has nearly 250 similar quotes on the topic of learning from our mistakes. In this chapter, I'll focus on some of the mistakes I've seen and experienced. Many of these lessons can be applied by counter-trafficking professionals who are seeking to be the best they can be.

Walk the talk

I was invited to a dinner at a major human rights advocate's home. I was very excited. For me, this was a great honour. For nearly two years, I had heard of the groundbreaking work that Ram (not his real name) had carried out across Nepal.

I attended this event with a diplomatic officer from the US Embassy.

At Ram's home, we shared some simple finger food and tea as we discussed his latest move to place a new human rights law in front of the parliament. I listened to his every word, basking in his brilliance and immense experience. I had seldom met a person with more legal knowledge on any topic.

After our first cup of tea, our host pressed a device to summon his house staff from the kitchen. After ringing the bell twice without a response, a child, who appeared to be around ten years old, entered the room. He was dressed in a clean, simple village outfit. His expression betrayed his fear. Our host scolded the child for his tardiness with a series of exaggerated hand gestures as he barked a few orders in Newari, a language I didn't understand. The child rushed off.

Five minutes later, he came back with a full tea service. After putting the tray down, he poured the tea with trembling hands. When it came to my cup, he accidentally spilled it all over the table.

Without hesitating, our host slapped the child across his chest, grabbed his arm hard, and shouted a reprimand for his clumsiness. The fear in that boy's eyes told the whole story. This was not an isolated incident. Without missing a beat, the man turned and said, 'I'm sorry you had to see this. He is forever spilling things. He is a stupid child.'

In South Asia, there is a long tradition of taking children from villages and having them come to the city to work as domestic workers for well-to-do families. In the best of circumstances, these children are given an education or a future livelihood. But, all too often, they sadly instead become a family's live-in slave. In exchange for food and board, they are expected to work from dawn to dusk. For many, it is a form of forced child labour because they have no choice in the matter.

When a US government diplomat comes in contact with an abusive situation like this, it is not uncommon for them to leave. This is exactly what followed. I could tell that Ram did not understand why we would leave so abruptly.

I don't know what happened to that child. We reported the incident to the leadership in the embassy but I never heard the outcome. I do know that Ram was never invited to come to the embassy again, and I also heard he couldn't understand what he did to bring this about. He did not make the connection between his own actions and their consequences.

While most people who work in our sector practice what they preach, this was an example of a so-called human rights advocate who had drawn a line between the 'big picture efforts' he worked on and his own personal conduct. He did not apply the same strict code to his own personal life. The sad part was that he couldn't see this.

On another occasion, I observed a similar example at a human rights conference in Cambodia. I arrived at the breakfast area early to get a jump on some work. A few minutes later, a prominent human rights leader from Europe arrived. He walked up to the section where the eggs were prepared and had to wait two or three minutes for the cook to finish a phone conversation.

At the first opportunity, he started to shout at the cook for making him wait. He continued his attack for several minutes until the manager came up to see what was happening. After explaining the situation, the manager dressed down the employee in front of everyone. This man was thoroughly embarrassed. I felt sorry for him. While the cook had perhaps acted unprofessionally, the matter hardly seemed to warrant such a strong response.

On my way out of the restaurant, I went up to the cook and said, 'I am sorry about what happened. It really shouldn't have been a big deal.' The man burst into tears. He explained that his wife was having an operation that day. He desperately wanted to be at the hospital, but no one could cover his shift. The call he took came from one of the hospital nurses. Had the human rights 'expert' exercised some patience and given the cook the benefit of the doubt, he might have discovered that this man desperately needed some empathy and compassion.

Lesson: It is important to live up to the standards we expect from others when we promote human rights. It is hypocritical to say one thing and do something else. If we are not patient, empathetic, compassionate, and principled by nature, the human rights sector is not the right field for us. We must walk the talk.

A wolf in sheep's clothing

In one of the countries where I lived and worked, the government hired a human trafficking advisor to provide advice and guidance across their ministries and departments. For this book, I'll call him David. David's role was to develop policies and put in place programmes to address the problem.

By this time in my career, I had worked with many experts. Most had a particular expertise that focused on a given topic, such as legal, prevention or protection. But there was something about David that was very remarkable. He seemed to have a grasp of every aspect of the topic that went beyond nearly everyone else I had met. While I felt I was pretty knowledgeable, I often found myself taking copious notes whenever he presented at a meeting, conference, or seminar. He was a very well-informed, intelligent, and articulate person who could captivate his audience with his many stories.

He had an uncanny ability to describe how the human trafficking process unfolded at a visceral level.

During my time working with David, he told me a story about a Russian mafia-run brothel network based in the USA. According to him, the people involved in this network were supposedly ex-KGB agents who were disenfranchised after the fall of the USSR. He offered detailed descriptions of the criminals, the victims, how they were recruited, what happened at these sex venues, and how they were able to hide the business. According to David, the network catered to high-net-worth individuals, politicians, and other VIPs who were willing to pay huge amounts to be with young prostitutes and underaged girls. I was so shocked by his story that I wrote a novel and screenplay to help expose it entitled *Just Beyond the Spider's Web*. While the novel was never published, the essence of this story was included in a screenplay that is now being considered for production in Hollywood.

During a major international human trafficking conference that I attended in the USA, David and I were both presenters. At the end of his talk, several women got up and started to shout at him. They accused him of being a human trafficker. Their unexpected outburst created a lot of chaos at this event. Having worked with David, I came to his aid. I couldn't understand how these people could attack a well-known trafficking expert. After a couple of years, David returned to Europe to complete a book and his PhD. On a number of occasions, he sought my insights on his theories and approaches, which I provided.

A few years later, a reporter contacted me and asked if I knew David. I responded yes. To my complete shock, she informed me that David had been arrested and sentenced to twelve years in jail for being a human trafficker. When he was working as an advisor, I learned he was actually hiding out to avoid some criminal charges that he was accused of in Europe.

When I looked back at my time with David, I realized that there were probably things about him that I should have picked up, but I didn't. When we accept a person in a particular role, we don't question how they got there. In fact, I recall that David wanted to assist a young girl to get a job in Europe as a domestic worker. This could have easily been a human trafficking event if it hadn't been stopped by the government.

When Jeffrey Epstein was arrested on human trafficking charges, I came to realize that David's horrific detailed description of the sexual enslavement of young girls to cater to the wealthy and powerful in Europe and North America mirrored his story.

Lesson: This is a good example of a wolf in sheep's clothing. It is important we understand that the criminal element can be found among us. If there are signs of unorthodox behaviour, we must look into this.

Shelter disaster

As more and more stories began to surface about the fate of Nepalese girls in Indian brothels, the press spent more time highlighting the problem. During one week, three articles profiled the horrors of the flesh trade. A series of opinion pieces followed, demanding that the Nepalese people address the problem.

Once the topic began to go mainstream, discussions and debates about what should be done took place. During a women's club meeting, a group of middle-class housewives read the articles and decided they needed to do something to help. After discussing it with their husbands and families, they pooled their money and rented a small house to act as a relief shelter. They aimed to take in up to five trafficking victims. They would provide food, shelter, job training, and healthcare. They spent weeks excitedly planning for the day when this would happen.

After hearing about my work, they invited me to share information about what to expect when trafficking victims returned from India. Encouraged by their enthusiasm, I visited the home.

The shelter looked wonderful. The beds were lined up with a nice pillow and freshly pressed sheets. The walls were newly painted. A small, wooden locker was placed at the end of the beds. A few stuffed animals had been placed on the beds.

After hearing the women's dreams of helping these people, I saw that they had a clear vision of how the girls' arrival would unfold. Five young girls wearing flower dresses would step out of the van and come running over to the women. These victims would cry the moment they saw their beautiful rooms. The stuffed animals would be scooped off the beds, and a round of hugs would follow. The women would soak up the moment and feel good about their role as saviours. When they talked about this upcoming meeting, I could almost see tears in their eyes.

After learning that a group of girls would be arriving the following week, I asked a few questions about their background. Most were now sixteen years old. They had been in the brothels for nearly four years. When I heard this, I wondered if their storybook meeting would happen the way the women had envisioned. After four years in the brothels, most of the girls return completely changed. Not all victims are young, submissive children in need of a mother's love. Some return cold and hardened by the lifestyle. Instead of turning against it, they eventually come to embrace it. After providing some simple suggestions, I left but agreed to return the following week.

When the van pulled up at the shelter, the air was full of joy and anticipation. The vehicle came to an abrupt stop on the dirt pavement, and a cloud of dust filled the air. After waiting a few minutes, the driver got out, came around to the van door, and opened it. As each girl stepped out, within a matter of seconds the mood completely changed.

Instead of five young, submissive girls in flowery dresses expecting a welcome hug, they turned out to be teenagers dressed in high heels, miniskirts or tight jeans, and revealing tops. One of them spat every few seconds. Others chomped on gum. From the moment they arrived, their facial expressions revealed their contempt and disdain.

When the welcoming committee walked up to them, both sides stopped, not knowing what to do. After a short, awkward speech, the girls were escorted into the shelter to see their new space. One girl jumped onto the first bed she saw, pushing the stuffed animals onto the floor. An argument broke out over who should get the bed closest to the windows. Two of the girls faced off with shouting, pushing, and foul language. This exchange revealed their true nature. They were coarse, crude, and unrefined in every way.

No one had prepared the sheltered housewives for this potential outcome. Since brothel life is filled with drugs, alcohol, swearing, fighting, surviving, and worse, this lifestyle completely changes a person. While these young women had probably been docile and sweet at one time, they were now street-hardened from their atrocious experiences. Before their arrival, they were used and abused by everyone around them.

To survive, they acclimated—they took on the spirit of the life they had been forced to live.

After walking into the sewing room, one of the ladies explained that each girl would be taught how to sew. One girl laughed out loud and said, 'They expect me to learn to use that thing? Are they kidding? They want me to sit and sew for ten hours a day when I can walk outside that door right now and make 500 rupees in twenty minutes?' The room fell silent. No one knew what to say.

While I never revisited the shelter, I learned things went from bad to much worse. With each passing day, the girls became more rebellious and unruly. They refused to be exposed to anything that might help them improve or learn a new skill. They slept until noon, stayed up until 3:00 a.m., played loud music, drank whisky, and regularly shouted at each other. All they wanted to do was go outside the compound, make money, meet boys, and party.

As the days passed, the women who set up the shelter prayed for some way to escape this nightmare. They reached out to other shelters to see if they would accept the girls. But by then, word about this wild bunch had been broadcasted. The shelter workers' dreams of being saviours to some young, helpless victims completely disappeared.

Two weeks after arriving, the girls wandered off. When the last girl left, the shelter doors shut and never reopened.

Lesson: It is important to know about the world we live in. Our expectations may not always match the world that exists.

Falling in love with our saviour role

During one of my trips to China, I took a train from Nanning to Guilin. I love trains and was very excited.

I sat by the window, anticipating the wonderful views of the countryside.

Sitting in the seat in front of me was a young, loud Australian college student, who spent nearly an hour talking with her friend about how wonderful she was for spending a week volunteering at an orphanage in Cambodia. Nearly everything she said focused on her 'sacrifice' and 'immense contribution.' She said, 'Not too many people would do what I did. I spent a week of my life helping these poor people. They were really lucky to have me there. I could tell I reached them as a role model. I doubt they ever had anyone as good as me there.'

As I sat listening to her go on and on about herself, I felt she had completely missed the point. Sometimes volunteers forget the most fundamental objective of their service. It is not about them; it is about the people they serve. This person fell in love with herself as a saviour. By doing this work, she felt excessively noble and self-important.

We have all seen examples of this: the person who haughtily states that they are working to fight oppression or slavery or injustice in a manner that places the emphasis on themselves. Sometimes a self-satisfied smile goes along with this, as they wait for recognition or a pat on the back for being so wonderful.

Sadly, I have sometimes acted the same way. In my younger years, especially, I often lost sight of the victims I was supporting because I was too focused on my own nobility. When I remember that behaviour, I feel embarrassed and ashamed. I cringe over it.

Lesson: We must understand that when we volunteer to help others, we must do a job. We are there to serve, not to glorify ourselves. It is about them.

The wrong message can kill

Sometimes a misunderstanding, along with a confused message, results in a person getting hurt. This happened several times during my stay in Bangladesh.

To help prevent people from getting trafficked, a local NGO ventured into remote villages to inform these communities about the problem. Those teaching the course described traffickers as strangers from India who came to their communities to stalk young, unsuspecting girls. They stated that traffickers would lure their girls with false promises about good jobs and good money. They would convince the girls, then whisk them off to a brothel. With several girls missing over a two-year period, the community took this information to heart. They formed a community watch to look out for these predators.

Several months after the training, I heard that a travelling cosmetic salesman had ventured into this village. He stood by the school and tried to entice the girls to buy his products. Because his salesmanship sounded alarmingly like a trafficker's ploy, several community members became concerned. A fight broke out, and the man was beaten to death.

In this case, an unsubstantiated accusation resulted in a man losing his life. This was not the intent of the training. The message of how to properly handle suspected traffickers hadn't been clearly addressed. As a result, a person only suspected of being a trafficker became the unwitting victim of vigilante 'justice'.

Also missing from the training was the important caveat that many traffickers are not strangers. One Bangladesh study surprisingly found that more than half of the traffickers come from within a community itself. They manipulate and use what they know about a victim's home situation to convince the person to follow them.

Lesson: It is important to understand the facts about a problem. Half-truths and taking law enforcement matters into one's own hands can have a devastating outcome. Furthermore, a review of the data related to human slavery tells us that many traffickers don't come from outside—they stalk their victims from within.

Making false assumptions

During the time I worked in Bangladesh, we spent millions of dollars on a nationwide human trafficking prevention programme. At the time, Bangladesh had a population of over 140 million people. Because most of this population lived below the poverty line, we naturally assumed that most communities would be vulnerable to modern slavery. What was our rationale? If people are poor, they are desperate. We assumed that this desperation would result in them making bad decisions that would significantly increase their chances of being trafficked. For many years, this assumption was accepted as a given. Poverty was the main contributing factor to trafficking. This idea seemed so logical and rational that we took it for granted.

Three years into our programme, we decided to do an evaluation. We interviewed several hundred known trafficking victims with the aim of understanding where they came from, how they got trafficked, where they were trafficked to, and how they got out of the situation.

The outcome of this study was surprising. The major findings revealed two significant conclusions. Most of the victims were not the poorest of the poor, as we had expected.

These people tended to be so poor that they didn't have the resources to enter the migratory pool, so they remained in their own villages. Most migrants need at least some resources to begin a migratory journey. What we found was that the emerging middle-class was the more vulnerable group. As some families began to prosper, they acquired a taste for prosperity. It resulted in them taking bigger risks with their family members.

Second, there were only three locations that were trafficking hotspots—Jessore, Dhaka, and Cox's Bazaar. While we had spent years talking about vulnerability factors in villages, we found that, in most cases, you could find two villages that had nearly the same characteristics with one difference—one had a history of human trafficking, and the other did not. What did we learn from this? If you want to understand where trafficking vulnerability exists, go to where it is already happening. This was one of the most relevant factors.

Armed with these findings, we completely changed our prevention programme, refocusing on middle-class communities in known hotspots. This allowed us to significantly increase our success rates because we had an approach that targeted those in need. While poverty was certainly a vulnerability, it was often one of several related factors, including a desire to experience the world, a hunger to earn more money, and unrealistic expectations about migratory processes.

When this research was presented at several conferences, there was significant resistance. Once an assumption has been accepted as a given in an academic community, getting people to give up their beliefs is never easy. After a presentation on the topic, one person angrily said to me, 'Are you telling me that your study is enough to change the way these 200 participants feel about poverty's dominating role in modern slavery? Are you telling me you know better than all these people who agree with me?' My response to this statement was direct but polite: 'I am completely open to your views, but please back them up with some data, and then we can talk.' He had little to say in response.

Lesson: There is no substitute for good data. While we might sometimes think we understand a topic, even the most logical assumptions should be backed up with data to support them.

Growing from failures

There are two quotes from John Dewey, an American philosopher and educator, that sum up the objective of this chapter: 'We do not learn from experience, we learn from reflecting on experience.' And, 'Failure is instructive. The person who really thinks learns quite as much from his failures as from his successes.'

If you're seeking a career in counter-trafficking, these lessons can be applied to your work, your personal relationships, or any other part of your life. When mistakes are made by others, they teach us to clarify what we really want and how we want to live. They also teach us to accept ourselves, despite being flawed and imperfect. On the other hand, focusing on others' successes teaches us the value of being persistent in the face of seemingly insurmountable obstacles. Success also helps us to affirm that our efforts can be helpful, impactful and worthy of continuing.

Chapter 11

Lessons From Personal Struggles and Experiences

The German philosopher Friedrich Nietzsche once said, 'That which does not kill us, makes us stronger.' In my own life, this statement has always been true. By experiencing difficulties, people build up their strength for the next, possibly more painful, event that may occur.

Tears

At a conference one day, something unexpected and extraordinary happened when I took part in a panel discussion alongside two other counter-trafficking responders and a facilitator. That day, I felt really on-message. My answers to the questions were direct and on target. I felt pleased with the outcome.

Near the end, the facilitator asked one last question: 'How do you deal with all of the pain and sorrow you come in contact with?' The first person on the panel answered the question as most would: simply and practically, with little sentiment.

The second panelist did something that I almost never see at such times. He was triggered and broke down and cried as he described the sorrow he felt over the many terrible experiences he had encountered and the time he spent away from his family. I sat there thinking, 'I'm glad that's not me.'

When he finished, the moderator turned to me and asked, 'Matt, how do you deal with these issues?' A wave of memories flashed through my mind—faces of victims I had seen over the years. And all at once, I felt an incredible urge to cry. I could feel it coming, first at the pit of my stomach, then rising up into my head. I knew with every word I spoke, the urge grew more and more compelling.

I started bawling. I couldn't stop myself. The room went silent. No one knew what to do. Most people who heard me speak commented on how controlled I was in my presentation style. They described me as diplomatic and State Department-like. And yet, here I sat crying.

Not knowing what else to do, I kept my statement short. But the episode didn't end there. The moderator commented on ways this work affects us; how things build up and then just spill out. She asked the panel to respond to this. Once again, the same outcome followed. I choked through my words as I sat weeping in front of 150 people. I felt so embarrassed.

As the event ended, I wanted to run out of the room and hide. But something very interesting followed. Before I could get up, many people in the audience rushed up and offered their support. Compassion seemed to fill the air. Several people commented that it was one of the most 'real' sessions they had ever seen. Through our weeping, we showed our humanity. We revealed raw emotions that touched the audience to the core. It allowed the message to reach levels far beyond most academic presentations.

What caused those tears? I think many of us who are involved in this work tend to keep much of the pain and sorrow behind fortified walls in our minds. This is how we prevent ourselves from feeling too much. Most of the time, these walls hold firm, but sometimes things happen to break through that wall.

That moderator's question somehow pierced my emotional dam. I recognized then that I carry around a good deal of unresolved emotional pain. Probably, this pain comes from sorrow for the victims, as well as frustration that festers from our difficult work. Once my aching was exposed, I realized I needed to remove the walls to allow the hurt to heal. I also realized I must forgive myself for not helping more people. This is an irrational burden that activists often carry.

Lesson: Something powerful happens when we humble ourselves and show our true, unedited vulnerability in front of others. We reach people in a way that few things in life are able to replicate. We should never be afraid of showing our true emotions. Everyone feels things. We all experience extreme emotional states. It is not a weakness to show it; in fact, it is a strength.

Their shoes

For years, I worked in public health in a range of countries. Often it was my responsibility to visit hospitals and clinics and ask the person in charge for tours, review their files, or inspect the facilities. While many facilities had patients waiting, I seldom paid much attention to them. I also didn't focus much on the concept of patient care. I was more concerned with management and administration, not the people involved. I never seemed to have time for this. I carried out my visit, hopped in the land cruiser, and drove to my next site.

Two years after arriving in Bangladesh, at a reception, I suddenly dropped to the ground. I had no warning. My legs simply gave out. What I had was called a 'drop attack'. For several minutes, I couldn't feel my lower limbs. Gradually, sensation returned, and my legs came back to life. That night, I went home feeling apprehensive. I tried telling myself that this had been a freak event of no real consequence.

The next morning, my legs felt weak and shaky. I also experienced periodic bouts of dizziness. Alarmed, I went to the embassy medical unit. They asked me to wait a few days and see what happened next. During the next two weeks, things went from bad to worse. I couldn't stand for long, and my legs always felt unsteady. The spells of dizziness continued.

The embassy physician sent me to Singapore for tests. When no one there could identify the problem, I was referred to specialists in the United States. I feared that I might have multiple sclerosis—something serious and sometimes even fatal.

Before then, I seldom became sick enough to require medical care. I exercised regularly and ate well. Then, all at once, I found I might have a disease that would change everything—my ability to function, to get around, to grow old.

Something interesting happened during my visits to countless doctors. For the first time, I found myself on the receiving end of the healthcare system. I was the patient. I had to wait like everyone else, endure the administration and bureaucracy, and experience both good and bad bedside manners of the medical staff. At times, as I sat alone in the waiting area, the fear of what might happen next consumed my thoughts. With my confidence at an all-time low, a good day was when the system worked—the healthcare providers were friendly, attentive, and willing to answer questions. When these things didn't happen, it had a devastating effect on my mood.

Eventually, the issues with my legs resolved themselves without me ever knowing what happened, but what I learned in those hospitals stayed with me. For the first time, I realized how so much of a patient's recovery is tied to their mental state. The medical system affected that, both positively and negatively. Now I could understand how terribly frightened anyone suffering a health crisis can feel. We need the healthcare workers to understand us and show us compassion, kindness, and patience. I recalled with horror my insensitivity to patients during my clinic inspections. As a consequence, I dramatically changed the way I conducted health facility visits.

Lesson: We must put people ahead of business procedures, especially when dealing with those who are sick or with those who have been trafficked. We need to open our hearts and take time to understand the world from their perspective. Compassion and empathy can be our best teachers through life.

My cancer journey

In October 2017, my wife and I went together to see my urologist. Following a year of concerning symptoms, a PSA test that was abnormally high, and a biopsy, we went in to receive the results. Since he extended the period of time set aside for this appointment, I expected the worst. I walked into his office with my wife's hand in mine. We sat down. The expression on his face prepared us for what was to follow—it was stern and serious. He came right out and said it: 'I have bad news—you have prostate cancer.'

For anyone who has ever received this news, the shock of hearing those words stay with you forever. After the initial blow sunk in, we both asked a series of questions: how serious is it? What needs to be done? When does this all need to happen? After listening to the various treatment options, which seemed to proceed from bad to worse, we left the office and walked home in silence.

While I thought we might both break down, this reaction didn't happen immediately. We talked about what we might do in a logical, practical manner. It all seemed very matter-of-fact at first.

But as time went on, the reality of my situation began to surface. Over a six-month period, I found myself having many ups and downs. One day I was consumed with fear, then the next day I was depressed. On one occasion, I drank an entire bottle of brandy to escape from the myriad of emotions I was experiencing. I was acting out.

As hard as it was for me, I feel it was even harder for my wife. I had time to come to terms with my own situation. I spent months accepting my fate. But Sylvia was left with a scenario that she had no control over. I realized that for something like this, an entire family is affected in many ways. Everyone needs support. Everyone needs to be comforted.

As the operation date was approaching, my anxiety continued to increase. Since our family had a predisposition for blood clots—in fact, a simple operation killed my eighty-year-old mother—I went into the operation not knowing whether I would survive. In preparation, I spent weeks pulling together all of my papers, preparing a binder, and putting a will in place. It was a very sobering process.

The day arrived. Sylvia was beside me. The doctor came and gave me a sedative. I was wheeled away. The last thing I remember was being in the operating room, surrounded by many medical staff going through the various pre-operation processes. Then my world went blank.

I opened my eyes. I could feel myself being wheeled away. I had survived. I was dizzy and dry vomiting from the anesthesia. I was taken into my room. Sylvia was there, and I could see the relief on her face.

Four hours after the operation, my surgeon, Dr Wong, came into the room. After proudly showing us a picture of my prostate and two lymph nodes he had removed, he told us that the operation had been successful. But he admitted the cancer was more aggressive than he had anticipated, and he said that it could possibly return.

For anyone who has had their prostate removed, the recovery is long and hard. I had a catheter for nearly two weeks. Having a gland removed from that area of a man's body is traumatic. The adjustment took many months. But I was alive. My marriage life has also been profoundly enriched as my wife and I no longer take our time together for granted. While the anxiety and angst return every six months when I go in for my PSA test to see if I'm clear of cancer, I always walk away feeling grateful that I'm still alive.

Lesson: Facing the possibility that I might die from this disease completely changed me. It helped me come to terms with my own mortality. It helped me to understand that life was precious and that every day was a blessing. It helped me to put my priorities in order—my wife, my sons, my family, and my personal network. While I wouldn't wish this on anyone, it did offer me a completely new outlook on life; one in which I came to cherish the little things. In this way, I am grateful for the experience.

Facing our fears

One of my two lifelong fears is public speaking. These days, I do some 150 public speaking events a year. In the past, I would do anything to avoid this dreaded task.

I can trace the origin of my fear to an event that happened in the third grade. We were assigned to write two paragraphs about Abraham Lincoln. Since I was a student who completed tasks the morning they were due, I took a shortcut and copied two long paragraphs directly from the encyclopedia. I felt confident despite my wrongdoing.

When our papers were returned the next day, mine was marked unsatisfactory, but this was not the end of it. My teacher asked me to stand up. When I did, she asked if the text I had written was my own. I said yes. Of course, I lied. She asked me again. I said yes, a second time.

She told me to read my paper to the class. I knew I was in trouble. I looked at the essay and realized that I didn't understand many of the words I had copied down. Since the content was beyond my reading ability, I couldn't do it. Having no other choice, I began to read, often fumbling upon many of the words. Every time I looked up at her, hoping she'd allow me to stop, she told me to go on. Clearly, she was making an example of me.

From that moment, I developed a terrible fear of public speaking. If I couldn't get out of a required speaking assignment, I spent days before the event with unrelenting fear and a multitude of mini panic attacks. Like most people, I allowed my fear to control me. Most fears, like mine, are irrational.

My work in development required me to deliver presentations on a regular basis. But even decades after third grade, I still suffered with each talk. Instead of getting easier, it got worse. The anxiety, trepidation, and loathing took control of my life.

About ten years ago, I thought about the innumerable people who faced audiences every day. What was I so afraid of? Something had to change. I decided to fight my fears. I was tired of the fear controlling my life.

Finally, whenever presentation volunteers were needed, I stepped up. While my heart would say, 'Don't do it,' my mind took control. The process was not easy, but something amazing happened. While I never eliminated all fear, my public speaking started to improve. Now I realize that fear is an important ingredient for a passionate speaker. Fear helps fuel my passion for the topic, inspiring my words, and giving them more emotion and power.

Lesson: Our fears are sometimes self-generated. Often, they are based on past events that hold us back. Facing our fears may seem difficult and frightening, but the payoff is unbelievable. Fear can also be used to fuel our passion.

Speeches

As a continuation of the topic listed above, I'd like to describe some of the experiences I've had as a public speaker. Over many years, I have made hundreds of presentations on human trafficking and modern slavery. When I stand before a group, I never know what might happen. Sometimes, I feel the entire audience holding onto my every word. The words flow, the stories and supporting information contain the right balance of content and emotion, and the pace is right. Other times, I fumble over my words, the stories sound bland, and I sense the audience is not at all interested. A good indication of this is when mobile phones are pulled out. Perhaps it is a combination of the time of day, my level of tiredness, and my confidence at that moment.

Here are some of my more memorable speaking engagements:

- I made an hour-long presentation to an audience of about thirty people who listened intently to everything I said. In the end, I found out that none of them spoke a word of English.
- In Bangladesh, I spoke to 500 people who I knew didn't understand what I was saying. There was no interpreter. While I had prepared a set of talking points for the audience, it made no difference what came out of my mouth. I was there as a foreign diplomat. Protocol dictated that I had to say something. I could have talked about my recent vacation, and they still would have clapped.
- I went to a university, expecting to do a one-hour presentation. When I arrived, the professor told me that he didn't want a presentation; he'd prefer to interview me. While this was unexpected, I agreed. Within a few minutes, he was making provocative statements and firing challenging questions at me. After realizing this was an ambush, I adjusted my thinking and told myself, 'Bring it on, dude.' I found that format to be an excellent way to get information across. Both the professor and the students lobbed tough questions my way. It became a tremendous learning experience for us all.
- At a church event, where I expected thirty people to show up, only one person came. The church dropped

the ball on informing their audience. I gave the presentation anyway.

- At one presentation I gave, half the people fell asleep. Every few minutes, another one dropped off. Frustrated and to emphasize a point, I slapped the board, and ten people popped to attention.

- During a speech in Singapore, I was heckled the entire time. An older British man repeatedly said 'Humbug' throughout the talk. When the question-and-answer period came, he said, 'You do-gooder types are always making up these stories about problems that don't exist. There are no slaves in this world today.' When he wouldn't stop his rude comments, one of the organizers stepped in. After the presentation was over, I asked him to read some materials. He refused. I asked again, and he finally agreed. Two weeks later, I received an apology stating that he was wrong. He checked the information and came to understand that the problem was real. It was a big breakthrough.

- A woman told me once that my talk was no good. She said she didn't cry much; most other talks made her cry more. Mine didn't, so to her, it was a bad presentation.

- An African American woman told me that what I was doing was an affront to the 'real slavery' that took place in the US. By equating human trafficking to slavery, she said I was evil and insensitive. She was so frustrated with me that I felt she might slap my face at any moment.

- At an international Rotary conference in Thailand, the meeting was scheduled for two hours, but when I finished my speech, they asked me to continue talking. After sharing a second PowerPoint, they asked me to keep going. My presentation continued for nearly four and a half hours.

I try to maintain a delicate balance when I do presentations. It took a long time to figure this out, but once I did, I realized its importance. If I make the content too sad or depressing, the audience gets so overwhelmed with despair that they become almost comatose. Instead of engaging, they withdraw. On the other hand, if I talk about the problem in a less serious manner, they feel I am insensitive. The ideal is to begin with serious stories and end with a hopeful message. An optimistic closing is a must for a successful talk.

Some groups we address are easier to engage with than others. Fifth graders are one of my favorite age groups. They are fearless when it comes to asking questions. Some of them challenge my expertise. If I really want to hone my skills, I take on one of these classes. They have not yet reached that age where they are concerned about what people think of them. Middle school is the hardest group because it is nearly impossible to get them to ask questions. They are so self-conscious about boy-girl issues.

One time at a Hong Kong high school for boys consisting of tenth and eleventh graders, not a single person asked a question. Frustrated, I asked how many of them wanted to go to university. All hands were raised. I asked if the competition was hard. They all nodded their heads. I gave a short lecture on how universities value proactive students who raise questions. I also said this could decide whether a person was accepted. Within five seconds, the hands started flying up in the air.

Different requirements require different approaches. For most Western audiences, I start by saying I will be talking about human slavery, then offer some case examples and continue with basic information. This method usually works well with this audience.

For Asian populations, this approach seldom works. If I announce I will be talking about human slavery first, many completely close their minds. They consider slavery to be something that happened in the past—something that no longer exists. We show that it does as we describe a series of case examples focusing on known exploitation scenarios readily found within Asia, and I sometimes mention the historical example of military sexual servitude by the Japanese military during World War II. At the end of this description, I say that this is what we now call modern slavery. This simple change in order makes a big difference.

Now and then, I'll have a student offer a personal challenge. It seems like they want to take on the expert. One girl said, 'Your suggestion that there are 500,000 slaves in the US is ridiculous. The State Department's Trafficking in Persons Report clearly states that the number is about 60,000. It was wrong for you to make this statement.'

My response is usually simple but direct: 'The Trafficking in Persons Report draws upon available data. Like all of these numbers, the information is incomplete and sometimes inaccurate. I base my estimation on reports I have seen and my personal experience. This was my own opinion. Do you have information beyond the TIP report to substantiate your concerns? If so, I'm willing to hear what you have to say.' Sometimes my response has a negative effect, seeming to hurt the questioner's feelings. This is never my intention.

At the end of my presentations, often a small group surrounds me. Some thank me for my talk, while others ask a question or offer a comment. Although most of them ask for my card and promise to contact me later, few follow through. A presentation like this opens their heart for a time. The people standing before me sincerely want to help. But within a short while, they go back to their old world as if the talk never happened.

Lesson: Presenting information in the form of a speech is one of the best ways to increase awareness. For a successful talk, it is important to be well prepared and able to answer questions. Following each presentation, it's important to collect feedback and analyze what went well or could be improved. This analysis can help me to engage participants to become better advocates in the fight against modern slavery. In general, this introspective approach can also be used for any and all lessons. By applying them to our future activities, it will contribute to our counter-trafficking efforts or the efforts of others.

Differing audiences

When I shifted from working with the development sector, which included governments, NGOs, and the United Nations, to working with the private sector, I had to make some significant changes. There are some major differences between the working styles, approaches, and expectations among different sectors.

This fact became readily apparent during one of my early donor meetings in Hong Kong. Through a mutual friend, I was asked to do a presentation to three prominent corporate officials. Armed with my PowerPoint deck that contained eighty-seven well-crafted slides, I began. After the fifth slide, one of the participants turned to me and asked, 'Are you almost done?' I was a bit shocked.

I learned an important lesson that day. In the NGO world, our programme pitches are often long and detailed. We walk our audience through a meticulous set of assumptions, rationales, objectives, activities, supporting data, and the like. Anticipating pushback from the participants, we try to address every aspect of our proposal with supporting data and research. Content is key.

The private sector often looks at the world differently. They assume the person making the pitch knows what they are doing and expect a summary of the problem—what is not working, and what needs to be done. One of the participants stated, 'Tell me what is broken and what needs to be done to fix it.' Another participant said, 'I am giving you this one chance to convince me. So convince me. But make it quick.'

The outcome of this meeting didn't go as I had planned. My typical NGO approach was not appreciated or accepted, and I walked away with nothing. But the experience helped me understand that I needed to retool myself.

Another thing that contributed to my 'NGO-ness' was the way I presented myself. For nearly ten years, I had a habit of wearing polo shirts at work. During my time at the United Nations, my shirt had a UN emblem. When I shifted to the Mekong Club, I had shirts made that featured our logo. For the first three years, I wore these shirts to all of my meetings. As much as my staff told me that I needed to wear a button-down shirt with a tie, I resisted. I felt it was inconsistent with who I was. In reality, I did this because I had a rebellious attitude.

But over time, I realized that this approach was a liability. Because I refused to conform to this new world, I could tell that people thought I was the delivery man instead of a professional development worker. This reality was most apparent when I went to a venue to offer a keynote speech.

Upon arriving, I'd stand off to the side, and no one would approach me. I appeared to be a fish out of water in this environment. It was only after my speech that they realized who I was and why I was there.

One day I had had enough of this reaction. I woke up, put on a shirt and tie, and from that point on, things changed quickly.

In the early days working in Hong Kong, I always felt like an outsider. My NGO roots made me different. But over time, I replaced my spots with stripes, and now most of my private sector counterparts feel I am one of them. I now know how to talk the talk and walk the walk.

Lesson: To engage with different communities, we need to conform with their norms. I realized that this didn't change who I was; it simply changed the potential for me to get my message across without any distractions.

Anti-slavery campaign speaking tours in America

In May 2011, as I helped set up a US-based counter-trafficking campaign titled 'Breaking the Links', I had a crazy idea. Instead of our usual summer vacation with my two sons hiking, fishing, and hanging out, what if we took a road trip to different locations in the US and worked as a team to inform Americans about the issue, learn from them, and raise some money for the human trafficking cause? I proposed my idea to Brandon, seventeen, and Damien, fifteen, not knowing what to expect. To my surprise, they agreed immediately.

Between 29 July and 6 August, the three of us visited seven cities and gave twelve presentations introducing the Breaking the Links campaign. The venues included schools, libraries, churches, a theatre, a golf club, and a manufacturing centre.

In addition to reaching nearly 1,000 people with our message, we also raised nearly $10,000 to contribute to the cause.

For much of the trip, I was a dad beaming with pride. The experience offered a chance for all of us to see new sides of each other. My sons got a taste of my work and my world. I had the privilege to see them experience new things and grow in their roles. Brandon, my oldest, has a natural gift for public speaking. He is comfortable on stage and knows how to engage the crowd. He and I co-presented. Damien, the younger, became our road-trip manager. He managed the registration table, handled all logistical arrangements, and kept everything moving. His warm, friendly personality helped convince people to get involved.

One morning in April 2016, I woke up and decided that I needed to do it all again—this time a 100-day road trip across the US to teach corporations about human trafficking. My plan was to do one presentation a day during this extended period. Armed with this crazy idea, I went to my board and told them about my plan. To my surprise, they said no. I approached them a second time. They said no. I approached them a third time. They said no. I approached them a fourth time, and they said maybe. I wore them down. In the end, they agreed to thirty days. It turned out to be a seventy-day speaking tour.

Because I couldn't do this trip alone, I went to my wife and said with a big smile, 'Honey, guess what, we are going to do a cross-country road trip throughout America. We will visit twenty-seven cities and get a chance to really see our country. It will be like an extended vacation. It will be my birthday present to you.' I thought I was so clever.

Hmmmm. So, we started our little adventure together in Vancouver. Within the first week of this epic journey, the reality of what I had committed to hit home—this was NOT going to be the fun vacation I had originally promised. Along with the endless driving, relentless searching for hotels, and unyielding speech preparation, there was also the constant struggle to make it to all the venues on time. My wife almost flew back to Hong Kong from Kansas City, but we somehow made it. Our rental car clocked up a whopping 10,000 miles.

To atone for this miscalculation, you can imagine how many additional birthday presents I needed to generate. Despite everything, we managed to do 117 presentations and reach over 5,000 people.

One of the main objectives of our road trips was to gain an insight into Americans' perceptions of human trafficking issues. We learned a lot at each site we visited. Few among our audiences knew much about the issue. While most had some knowledge, there was much they did not know or understand. The fact that human trafficking extended beyond prostitution came as a surprise to them. Most were shocked at the magnitude of the problem. When they learned there are more slaves in the world today than ever before, they were stunned. They felt these issues were far away and unrelated to them. Experts often cited Nepal, India, and Thailand as the locations where this problem prevailed. Few understood that it existed in the United States. We learned that, once informed, Americans responded to these issues. Once hearts were opened, they wanted to get involved and do something to help. At every place we visited, people offered assistance.

I subsequently carried out three additional intensive speaking tours: to Australia, New Zealand, and Canada. The rationale for these road trips was that modern slavery in these countries is a very sensitive topic within the private sector. Many companies didn't want to believe that it could be a part of their supply chains. Others recognized the problem but didn't know how to get started solving it. Still others were unsure of the quality of their anti-slavery systems relative to their peers, and they didn't know how to improve their policies and procedures. But with a range of new legislation related to modern slavery globally, increasing numbers of lawsuits against corporations, and wider media attention, ignoring this issue was not an option. Because this topic had not been addressed in a standard way, I decided to do these speaking tours to raise awareness and offer technical advice and guidance to a range of audiences.

Each of these events included trips to multiple cities. It was important to remember that many companies with significant Asian supply chains had head offices and management decisions being made in these countries, and engaging with their populations was key to creating global policies. The following testimonials resulted from this project:

> *'The presentation was very eye-opening. It addressed many details that our bank had no idea about. We will bring this information back to some of our working groups to determine how we can respond to this topic in a more efficient and effective manner.'*
>
> *– Bank representative*

> *'The presentation provided details to our company that were absolutely shocking. We now feel better equipped to understand the problem.'*
>
> *– Shoe manufacturer*

> *'We sent the presentation to our offices around the world. We will use this event to explore new ways to measure risk. This will help to protect our overall business.'*
>
> *– Fashion brand*

'Following this presentation, we reached out to our office in Hong Kong to set up follow-up briefings across Asia to make sure others in our company are educated and informed.'

— *Construction company*

'Following your presentation, we will regroup to decide how to include a component in our legislation that encourages companies to work with the government in a positive, supportive manner. We agree this emphasis is relevant and important.'

— *Canadian senator*

Lesson: It is important to test the waters to better understand what will and won't work. One of the best ways is to interact more often with both public and private audiences. This easy, direct approach can be done in a fun and exciting manner.

Helping hands—we can always find people who will help

Once in a while, something happens that appears to present an impossible problem. Years ago, I was driving my car along a remote Nepalese road. I rounded a corner, and the car stalled. I had broken down where I could be hit if a bus came barreling round the corner. I managed to pull my vehicle over to the curb to diagnose the problem. I failed to see a deep ditch in front of me. With no warning, my front tire dropped into the ditch, and the car stuck fast. After several attempts to drive it out, I realized I needed a big truck to pull me out. As I stood agonizing over my options, a local bus rounded the corner, slowed down, and stopped. Twenty men jumped out, gathered around the car, and pushed it out of the ditch.

I hadn't flagged them down. I hadn't called them over to help. It was spontaneous kindness and compassion. Once they had finished, they climbed into the bus, waved goodbye, and sped away. The whole thing took about six minutes. My head spun from this completely unexpected event that saved me untold hours of torment. What happened? The people on the bus saw my need and responded. They expected nothing in return. They performed this selfless act out of pure kindness.

This same concept works with mentoring. During my professional career, several inspiring individuals have taken me under their wing. Most did it because others had helped them at the start of their own careers. They said it was a way to thank those who had supported them and to pay it forward. I vowed to do the same for others when my turn came. And this, I do.

Lesson: We must anticipate opportunities to help others in need. This comes naturally to us, usually takes little time or effort, and genuinely helps the person who needs us. As someone who has received help often, I feel it is my honour and privilege to help others—in a spirit of gratitude to those who helped me.

Walking in the shoes of those we try to help

Years ago, three NGO/UN workers asked me to teach them what I knew about human trafficking. While I knew very little at that time, perhaps I had more knowledge and experience than most. After putting it off for nearly two months, I agreed to provide them with a session.

A few days before we started, I asked, 'What are you hoping to get out of this experience?'

Their enthusiastic answer was very specific: 'We want to walk away with a real understanding of the problem.'

Armed with this explicit request, I asked, 'Can we meet at your office on a Saturday morning?' They said yes. 'Will there be anyone there?' I asked. They said no. We agreed to meet at 10 a.m.

Upon arriving, I asked to see their storage room. The room had a padlock on the outside. Inside were a small table, a chair and a range of office supplies. 'Let's meet in this room,' I suggested. Despite the unusual request, they agreed. When they got settled, I walked out, locked the door outside, and left the building. They were trapped with no way to escape. This was before mobile phones.

For the next three hours, I had a nice lunch, made a few calls, and ran some errands. When I returned, I heard them pounding on the door and shouting for help. I opened the door and said, 'Now you understand. Now you know what it is like to have your life stolen. I controlled you for three hours. This, my friends, is the essence of human slavery—a loss of our personal freedom.'

Naturally, I got into a lot of trouble for this unorthodox stunt, and I don't recommend that anyone use this technique; however, the lesson did sink in. In later years, I met two of these men, and both talked about that day. Despite their anger at that time, they admitted there is no substitute for first-hand experience.

I also had experienced similar lessons. During my master's course at New York University, I was assigned the task of begging on the streets of New York City. I dressed in old clothes and ventured into the streets at night. The experience amazed me.

As a large, Caucasian, middle-class male, I am hard to overlook. But the moment I put my hand out to beg, I became the Invisible Man. People pretended not to see me and walked by as if I wasn't there. Sometimes they walked around me as if I was a post. I could not have understood what people begging felt had I not tried this. It changed my perspective.

Although plenty of people ignored me, I actually collected a great deal of money. A significant minority reached into their pockets and hastily handed over cash. I felt surprised at how relatively easy it was.

When I explained this to my professor, he sensed that I had approached the exercise incorrectly. He asked me to demonstrate my technique. I did as I was told. I walked up to him with my hand in front of me, looked him in the eyes, and asked for the money. He laughed. 'Don't you see?' he said. 'Those people gave you money out of fear. They saw this very large man with an intense gaze and thought you might rob them. Next time, do it with your head down, with no eye contact.' He asked me to try again. When I repeated the exercise, I became almost totally invisible.

Lesson: At times, we must walk in the shoes of those we hope to help. This brings empathy, understanding, and compassion, which adds value to our work. While our minds do a great job imagining the problems other people face, there is no substitute for first-hand experience.

Chapter takeaway

Many of the lessons outlined in this chapter are more personal than those in previous chapters which focused more on counter-trafficking initiatives, measures and historical trends. These anecdotes and stories were offered to help those who might be interested in doing anti-slavery work to apply them to their own efforts. This, I feel, will allow the reader to learn from my own personal struggles and experiences, which can help them be more effective in their future endeavours.

Chapter 12

Learning From Tools, Projects and Best Practices

In the previous chapter, I provided personal anecdotes and stories to reflect upon the lessons that I had learned from my own experiences. In this chapter, we will continue the journey, but this time, I will focus on some of the lessons learned from the tools and projects I encountered as part of my work. Along with the myriad of practical insights counter-trafficking workers learn as we move from nation to nation, city to village, researching and collecting data, and conferring with colleagues and governments, we can also discover many deep lessons related to the programmes we come in contact with.

Best practices generally represent positive activities or systems that a person recommends to others for use in similar situations. I will provide some examples of different tools, projects and activities I have developed or seen. The purpose is to highlight how creativity, innovation, and ingenuity can help to address a problem or make a programme more effective.

Mongolian prevention effort

For a prevention programme to be effective, it must meet three criteria. First, it must target the right people. Second, it should result in behaviour changes so individuals avoid being trafficked. Third, it should be cost-effective and replicable. A programme we instituted in Mongolia met each criterion with excellent success.

We had known for some time that young women from Mongolia were being trafficked through Japan and into Macau in China, where they were being forced into prostitution. After two or three years, some victims managed to return home. To avoid losing face, nearly all of them lied about their experience. The potential shame, embarrassment, and stigma were simply too overwhelming. If anyone found out what they had done, they would never get a husband.

How did this victimization process work? The back page of the local newspaper carried ads that said, 'If you are young, unmarried, pretty, and you want to make money overseas, contact us, and we will send you to Japan to work in a restaurant.' Since many young people find Mongolia to be isolated and boring, women would call, and after hearing they could make great money in an exotic location, they would accept the job. Once recruited, they were sent to Japan. But several weeks later, on a false pretence, they'd be trafficked into the brothels in Macau.

To help stop this problem, our proposed solution was simple. We bought a cell phone, put a lot of minutes on it, and hired a well-trained NGO worker to answer it. She was told to provide advice and guidance but never reveal who she was or name her organization. We then put an ad in the newspaper among the other false solicitations. This ad simply stated, 'Before calling anyone else about a job, call us first.' We provided no other information.

The calls soon came in. The young women would ask, 'Do you have a job for me?' The NGO person would say, 'No, but let me tell you about some of the other companies out there and what might happen to you if you sign up with them.'

This approach allowed us to help some people to avoid making a big mistake. Armed with this basic information, many were deterred from accepting false jobs. But something else happened. A second group of people called the same number. These were women who had been trafficked but never told anyone their story. Somehow, word got out about this 'hotline' that could help people who had been trafficked, and victims started to call. This information helped to significantly increase the number of cases known to the police.

Surprisingly, a third group also called—the traffickers. Their business had dropped off due to our efforts. After learning that our call service talked women out of accepting jobs abroad, these criminals began telephoning to threaten the NGO worker. Since we used a cell phone, we recorded the traffickers' numbers and gave them to the police. All in all, it was an efficient, inexpensive way to help innocent people from being horrifically exploited.

Lesson: We must find solutions that fit the problem. The best solutions reach people with the information they need, when they need it, before they make a tragic decision.

Innovation of a mobile phone app

Law enforcement officials throughout Asia often come into contact with potential slavery victims. However, because they cannot communicate with them and don't know which countries they come from, the victims go unidentified. This is particularly problematic in labour trafficking situations, including cases related to fishing boats and seafood packing. As a result, many slaves lose what is likely to be their only opportunity for rescue, and enslavers continue unhindered with impunity.

To help address this problem, in 2016, the Mekong Club and the United Nations University created a smartphone application that allows Asian regional law enforcement to use smartphones to question potential victims who speak another language. This tool demonstrates that technological solutions can be used to solve language problems in human trafficking.

The app can be installed on any Android device. To communicate with potential victims, the user presses an icon, which brings up a sample of flags on the phone's screen. The potential victim presses the appropriate flag, and an audio recording provides information about their rights in their native language. It assures confidentiality and explains that the officials playing the video to them are there to help.

A series of questions are asked during the video. Respondents are prompted to press the green button to answer yes and the red button to answer no. All of the yes responses indicate that there is a potential issue. The questions include: Have you been exploited? Do you need assistance? Do you want help? This helps law enforcement officials to determine if the respondent is a victim of human trafficking. Officials soon learned that some 20 per cent of those questioned were victims. In the first pilot of this tool, these victims would not have been identified without the app.

Despite the very encouraging results, one immigration officer in Thailand said, 'I will never use this tool because it reveals more victims, and this adds too much extra work. There are lengthy activities that have to be carried out when we come across trafficked persons.' This was an indirect way of saying the app was a success. Unfortunately, it also revealed his indifference to the plight of these victims.

In 2018, a second version of this app, named Apprise Audit, was developed for factory auditors. Social compliance audits are key to examining working conditions within factories and other facilities in supply chains. Within audits, workers' interviews are a critical, often compulsory component, providing the voice of the employees on working conditions. They reflect the only direct contact that auditors have with workers during their factory visit, and thereby represent an opportunity for workers willing to report on exploitative working conditions when grievance channels are inefficient or non-existent. The data collected during these interviews provides credible first-hand information on working conditions, highlights areas for further examination by an auditor, and helps to determine whether trafficking or exploitation exist in the workplace.

The problem is that if an auditor wants to interview a migrant worker from another country, they often don't have an interpreter there to collect this information. Then again, if the factory manager is nearby, this can intimidate the worker into silence.

The Apprise Audit app was developed with the aim to solve these challenges and improve auditors' detection of labour exploitation indicators during worker interviews. It is a multi-language mobile app downloaded on the auditor's phone and used to interview workers through an audio questionnaire. It works exactly the same way as the NGO version, allowing workers to answer yes/no questions in their own language.

The question list was created along with a group of stakeholders that included auditors, workers, brand representatives, and human trafficking experts. Apprise Audit flags indicators of vulnerability adapted from the International Labour Organization's 'Indicators of Forced Labour' list. Examples of ILO indicators include: deception, restriction of movement, worker isolation, physical and sexual violence, intimidation and threats, retention of identity documents, withholding of wages, debt bondage, abusive working and living conditions, and excessive overtime.

Following the interview session, workers' responses are uploaded and organized on a web-based server that can be accessed by companies to analyze and track factories' performances.

After the app was launched and tested, we conducted a field survey to observe its use during social compliance audits and to collect feedback from users. As part of this research, we concluded that the app contributed to enhanced victim identification processes and provided workers with a voice. It also empowered the brands and their suppliers to better understand the working conditions in their supply chains and make evidence-based decisions to remediate violations once they had been identified.

Two additional versions are being developed: one to identify potential red flags for exploitation in the domestic-worker community in Hong Kong, and another to address the COVID-19 crisis among workers throughout Asia.

Lesson: We must find every possible solution through technology and human ingenuity. Since most people have smartphones, these devices can be modified to address the problem.

Using drama to educate

As noted throughout this book, many trafficking victims are tricked and lured into going away with the trafficker based on promises of a job, a marriage proposal, or a better life. A major reason why these approaches are able to succeed is that the trafficking victims, their families, and their communities are unaware that these ploys even exist. One effective way to educate communities is through the use of a dramatic film. In Nepal, one example of this was a full-length motion picture titled *Chameli*. This two-hour film focused on a girl who was married to a man who eventually trafficked her to a brothel in Mumbai. The story depicts the brutality of the recruitment process, her journey to India, what happens at the brothel, and how she eventually escapes.

The reason I chose to fund this film was simple. For years, many activists had been working on issues related to child prostitution and trafficking girls in South Asia. Throughout this period, many organizations funded numerous studies to identify the scope of the problem using qualitative and quantitative research methodologies. Unfortunately, these studies tended to be too academic and didn't really capture the true essence of what was involved when a person was forced into prostitution. Second, most Nepalese people, especially villagers, don't tend to read these kinds of monographs. Therefore, the producer decided to try to describe what happens through the medium of drama. The idea was to develop an understanding of the problem and some empathy through the use of life-like characters who actually experienced trafficking as the story unfolded. This allowed viewers to understand the problem from not only an intellectual level but also an emotional one.

Chameli was a tale of love, life, corruption, and evil, and it provided a brief glimpse into a world seldom seen by outsiders—a world that is all too often much closer to home than we might want to admit.

The mastermind behind the film was Ravi Baral, one of the most compassionate, innovative, and creative filmmakers I have ever met and someone I consider to be a dear friend. The film Ravi created represented a number of milestones for Nepal. It was the first 'non-documentary' type film to deal with a serious subject. It was one of the few films out of South Asia that attempted to address this sensitive subject. The film won several international motion picture awards and ran for the longest time of any film in Kathmandu theatre history—seventy-nine consecutive days. It was also translated into Bangla and Hindi to be viewed across Bangladesh and India.

Chameli achieved many remarkable outcomes, including raising awareness of the topic, helping correct misconceptions about the traffickers, helping develop a sense of empathy and compassion for the victims, and having an impact on men who regularly used prostitutes. One man who was interviewed after an airing of the movie said, 'I wish I had never seen this story. I had no idea these women were forced into this profession. It is so unsexy to know this. I don't think I can go back to a place like that again.' Another man said, 'I felt so angry to think that those Indian men are using our girls. This has to stop.' Finally, one of the woman viewers admitted, 'I cried through the whole film. I had no idea this was happening. The film opened my eyes.'

Because the project had a shoestring budget, Ravi was forced to come up with innovative, cost-effective ways to produce the film. For example, through a family friend, he managed to transform an old palace located on the grounds of a Christian school in Kathmandu into a brothel site. The building and the street in front of it were transformed into an authentic, lifelike depiction of an Indian red-light district. About a hundred extras were brought up from the lower part of Nepal to add to the effect. I can only imagine what the students at that school thought about this change when they walked past it on their way to their classes.

As another cost-cutting effort, he recruited actors and actresses among people who had never acted before. After providing a month's training, they were cast into their roles. Another reason for this approach was that the director couldn't find any established actresses to play the roles of prostitutes. The reason for this attitude became apparent after the film was completed. The main star of the film, who played Chameli, was kicked out of her house by her father for playing this part. He felt it brought shame to the family. Following this outcome, Ravi paid for her university studies. She later went on to become a recognized movie star in Nepal.

Throughout my life, I have watched thousands of films. It is one of my favorite pastimes. But of all the films I've ever seen, the ending of *Chameli* was my favorite. There was something about Chameli's final act that still gives me chills.

During my career, I funded many similar projects. In Mongolia, I helped to produce a twenty-six-part educational soap opera focusing on HIV/AIDS. It was based on the tried and tested education-entertainment format that had been implemented in many countries globally—*Soul City* and *Sesame Street* being notable examples. In addition to increasing awareness of HIV/AIDS prevention among clients of sex workers, the series taught internationally accepted responses to such issues as stigma, HIV/AIDS in the workplace, care and support, and voluntary counselling and testing. It also addressed related issues such as human trafficking and health issues such as tuberculosis. The series was broadcast nationwide on Mongolian National Television over a six-month period with an estimated weekly audience of 500,000 citizens. In the post-broadcast period, the series was made available without charge for use in schools, universities, hospitals, libraries, and other public enterprises.

My wife, Sylvia, also used drama to tell her stories. As a gifted, award-winning filmmaker, she directed and produced two music videos that depicted sex trafficking scenarios based on songs that came from a human trafficking songwriting contest. Since some people are influenced by music, these dramatic depictions offered another creative way to raise awareness through emotionally impactful content.

Lesson: Using drama as a medium to educate is a tried and true intervention that works. It allows people to learn about a problem through the characters and the story that plays out on the big screen or television.

Bangladesh thematic group

As mentioned earlier in this book, in September 2002, an organization I regularly worked with, the International Organization for Migration, held a roundtable discussion titled 'Anti-Trafficking Initiatives: Bangladesh and Regional Perspectives'. Following a series of boring presentations, the group discussed and debated problems that existed in the trafficking sector. One person stated, 'I sometimes feel like we have the same meeting over and over again when we talk about trafficking. Within the first fifteen minutes, we end up arguing about the same things that have come up in past meetings. This is why I think we need to really sit down and sort out what we mean by trafficking once and for all.' Another person said, 'It is time that we look at what trafficking is after ten years of dealing with it. We need to be thinking about a "second generation" understanding of the trafficking problem.'

Following an in-depth discussion, the group concluded there were many inconsistencies in the existing human trafficking paradigm that had yet to be resolved in Bangladesh. The sector still lacked conceptual clarity, even among those who were working to reduce the problem. We needed to challenge some of our previous assumptions to restructure, revise and expand our understanding of the problem.

It was decided that a systematic process was to be adopted to formally 'come to terms' with trafficking in Bangladesh. A 'thematic group' would meet monthly to review various elements of the trafficking paradigm.

In the first session, a simple set of boxes and circles with text inside graphically initiated the discussion. Participants reviewed the diagram and suggested ideas that resulted in complete revisions. Subsequent meetings further refined the diagram.

The guiding principles for each session set by the overall thematic group were that the process itself was as important as the outcome, anything and everything should be questioned and debated until a consensus was reached, and there was no limit to what element of the problem could be introduced.

Over the next twelve months, a massive diagram grew to cover much of the wall. Each addition displayed a better understanding of the links throughout the trafficking process. One person said, 'I can now see the relationships between prevention and rehabilitation when I look at the matrix. I also see the elements that make up the problem.' Another person stated, 'After seeing the various elements that motivate a person to migrate, I can see that poverty is just one contributing factor. This will help us produce information campaigns to better tailor our messages.'

Each time the group revisited the matrix, they clarified unclear elements and suggested sharper approaches, ensuring the matrix more accurately reflected Bangladesh's trafficking realities.

This project yielded two vital outcomes—the invigorating process itself and the process's result. Discussions during the meetings proved invaluable. One participant stated, 'I really enjoyed these meetings. They helped me understand things that I was confused about.' Another said, 'This is the first forum where people who argued all the time could come to an agreement. Since elements are discussed logically and rationally, it is easier to get a consensus.'

The High Commission for Human Rights used the matrix while developing their 'United Nations Principles on Human Rights and Human Trafficking' document.

Even after nearly twenty years, there are few good at-a-glance visual tools, such as framework/matrix charts, that can provide lay people with an overview of human trafficking. Unlike reports that describe the problem using text, a framework or matrix can help us instantly understand the interrelated elements of a problem. This allows a group to be brought up to speed very quickly.

This process became one of the most important breakthroughs in my professional experience. It taught me that even the most diverse and divided professionals could unite when sharing mutual respect and common goals. I will always admire the Bangladeshi spirit, intellect, creativity, and sense of conviction. The country has some of the greatest thinkers in this world.

During this process, the person I relied on most was Shahidul Haque, the director of IOM Bangladesh at the time. Now and then in life, we all come in contact with extraordinary people. He was one of these people. Shahidul was one of the brightest, most articulate, compassionate, insightful people I had ever met. Always willing to do the right thing, he and I conspired together to make this process work. As a result of his belief in the process and in me, I will forever be in his debt. Years later, he went on to become Bangladesh's foreign secretary, a job that was both challenging and unforgiving. But with his immense sense of obligation and duty, he served his country well.

Lesson: It is important that we truly understand the problem we face. The best way to do this is to have regular discussions that unite a spirited group. While this adds time to the problem-solving process, it ensures a much better outcome. In this case, both the process and the outcome proved outstandingly valuable.

Sweatshop challenge

In the 1940s, Edgar Dale, a well-known American educator, proposed that we retain 10 per cent of what we READ, 20 per cent of what we HEAR, 30 per cent of what we SEE, 50 per cent of what we SEE and HEAR, 70 per cent of what we SAY and WRITE, and 90 per cent of what we DO. According to this theory, doing something is the best way to learn, and most of us have experienced this throughout our lives.

One way to reach people is to include them as participants in the story. For the past ten years, I have offered presentations on the issue of modern slavery to schools across the world. While most students appear to understand the basic details and the importance of the issue, with so much school content being taught on a daily basis, I wanted to see if we could offer an approach that would have more of a lasting impact. I began to show films that gave them a glimpse into the lives of trafficked persons. Seeing actual people in forced labour situations helped to increase their understanding of what the victims of trafficking endured. But even this content didn't have enough impact to significantly change the attitudes and behaviors of students, and I decided I needed to see if I could go even further.

The outcome of this was the Sweatshop Challenge. I developed this methodology to help students understand what it is like to be in an exploitative work situation. This simulation can be done with students ranging from 8th grade to seniors in high school. For every fifty students, there should be two volunteers acting as the sweatshop 'oppressors'.

This activity is usually done first thing in the morning. When the students arrive, they are immediately escorted to the gymnasium without an explanation. Upon entering, the organizers—my team and I—shout at them, 'Line up, stand in place, and don't talk.' They are given one nut and one bolt. They are then told that their classes have been canceled for the next five hours and they will stand in place and put the nut on and off the bolt for this entire duration. They are also instructed that if they talk, make eye contact with the organizers, or do it too slowly, they will receive an automatic detention.

For thirty minutes, the organizers give out detentions—even for arbitrary breaches or no breaches at all. Many of the students stand there not knowing what to do with themselves. They have never been in a situation where they are mandated to stand and do this kind of repetitive manual labour. The expressions on their faces often include bewilderment and confusion. Others become angry and frustrated.

At the end of this half-hour period, the students are told they can sit down, their classes will continue as scheduled, and they will NOT be receiving any detentions. The following statement is then made: 'Imagine if you had to do this work from 6 a.m. until 11 p.m. every day without a day off. Imagine if there was always someone standing there shouting at you, punishing you if you didn't do it fast enough. Imagine if this was your life. How would it feel? This happens to 25 million people around the world who are trapped in modern slavery. You only had to do this for thirty minutes. But what if this was your life?'

The remaining time is used to talk about how the students felt about the experience. What were their feelings and emotions? How did it feel to lose control of their time? This helps them to process the experience.

This interactive approach offers the students a powerful lesson. It gives them a taste of what many trafficking victims experience when they first find out they are under the control of others. Most importantly, it includes them in the story itself.

There were some insightful comments from these students:

> *I never did anything like this at school before. After doing this thing, I now know how it feels to be a victim.*

'The sweatshop activity was one of the most powerful lessons I ever had at school. I really thought I was going to have to stand there for five hours.'

'I was so afraid.'

'When I read stories about these people in slavery, I'll remember how I felt. It was really educational.'

'Had I not walked in their shoes, I wouldn't have understood. Now I do. For me, this changed everything.'

Later, one of the teachers reported, 'We do this every year now. It is one of our most talked-about events. The students really do feel changed.' Some students cried after the experience and a few told us that it inspired them to advocate to end forced labour.

At a school event, my wife and I met a mother of a thirteen-year-old girl who said her daughter's passion in life was to travel the world to rescue child slaves. She said she was taken aback by her daughter's transformed sense of purpose and her commitment to helping to end slavery after participating in this activity.

Feeling that we could go even further, I revised the methodology to offer what I called the Sweatshop Marathon. The goal of this exercise was to give participants a genuine taste of forced labour. The methodology had two objectives: to help raise awareness, and to help raise funding to fight the problem.

Volunteers were challenged to spend ten consecutive hours engaging in a repetitive action—putting nuts on bolts and then taking them off. During this activity, they were given no breaks, no food, no water, and no rest. It was done from 8 p.m. to 6 a.m. If they did not perform fast enough, they were scolded by the organizers.

Those who participated gained a real appreciation of how it feels to be in a forced slavery circumstance. After it was completed, the participants were asked, 'Imagine if this was your life seven days a week, 365 days a year. It isn't your life, and it shouldn't be anyone else's.' This tool has been used in Hong Kong and South Africa. Participants walk away completely changed. I've included some of their comments:

> 'I couldn't do it. I tried. I made it to four hours and that was enough. I can't imagine how people who are in sweatshop situations survive. It must be hellish.'

> 'I did the full ten hours. It was one of the hardest things I ever had to do. I can't imagine how awful it must be for those people who do this every day. It changed my life.'

> 'Before the challenge, I thought this kind of thing would be easy. No way. It is horrible, just horrible. Now I get it.'

It is hard to experience a Sweatshop Challenge and not feel a desire to help. Those who do it, feel their own pain. They feel the violation. They feel the need to speak out about this or to get involved.

Lesson: A good simulation gives participants greater knowledge of global challenges, engaging both their hearts and their minds.

Using virtual reality

Another way to help people experience a story is with new technology. Virtual reality offers a good example of this. As part of this approach, a 3D film is produced and then uploaded into a headset. The person watching the video feels they are actually sitting in the scene that is unfolding around them. We use these films to help sensitize business representatives about the topic of human trafficking. Since it isn't possible for us to bring them to the actual location, this technology is the next best thing.

At one of our business forums, we invited the corporate representatives to watch a short film on sex trafficking. The response was positive, and I share two of their comments here:

> *'Using virtual reality offers an emotive sense that comes from being in that situation and feeling and experiencing it. It is a very powerful way of helping people to understand a given reality.'*

> *'I feel this technology will help motivate more people at all levels to understand the relevance of this crime against humanity.'*

Lesson: While much of the focus of virtual reality has been on the gaming industry, it can also be an effective educational tool. The sensation of being in the VR environment can broaden ethical awareness, especially among banks, making it more real to a corporate crowd that doesn't really understand much about the world of human trafficking.

Role playing

One good way to help people understand how traffickers work is to do a role playing exercise using the audience. I ask if I can have five volunteers, and I send two of them to the other side of the room. I then assign roles to the three that are standing in front of me. I point to each of them and say, 'You will be the victim, and you will be the recruiter, and you will be the trafficker.'

With the 'victim' standing next to me, I turn to the audience and state, 'This person is the victim. She is in her village. She doesn't have a job and wants to get something more out of life.'

I then turn to the recruiter and say, 'This person is the recruiter. He's the one who approaches the victim and plants the idea of a job in her mind. He's the one who answers all of her questions and tells all of the lies.'

Pulling the trafficker over, I then state, 'Once the girl agrees to a situation, this person, the trafficker, takes the girl from her village to another location. Since she doesn't realize she has been tricked, she goes willingly.'

I then tell the person who played the recruiter to please sit down. I have the trafficker and the victim walk with me across the room to the location where the other two volunteers are standing. Once there, I ask the trafficker to please sit down.

I then make the following statement: 'This person here is the exploiter. He is the evilest one in this process. He is the one who owns the business that uses modern slavery. The person next to him is the enforcer. He is the one who beats and punishes the victims.'

After allowing the volunteers to sit down, I turn to the audience and say: 'All of these people are involved in the trafficking crime. Four of them are criminals. They all have a role to play. They all do bad things. They all need to be held to account.'

Lesson: By using this method, the audience is drawn into the story. Those who participate become partners in helping get my points across. This approach helps break up the talk. Anything that can alter the flow can be effective. It ensures that the presentation doesn't become repetitive or boring.

Chapter takeaway

As development workers, we can all use our imagination to look at issues and problems from different points of view. With creative ideas and innovation, we can overcome a range of obstacles. Creativity is a skill that can be developed and improved by questioning, experimenting, and moving forward with ideas, even if they don't seem too viable at first. A willingness to fail is a must in this process. But the reward can be amazing when new ways of addressing problems result.

Chapter 13

Some Theoretical Concepts

To complete this section of this book, I am including a few practical, theoretical concepts that have influenced my thinking and experiences over the past forty years. While some of them might appear to be abstract, in my own mind, they are very relevant to the work I do. They allow me to adjust my expectations in a way that helps me understand our world and maintain consistency.

My cat theory

Sometimes simple misunderstandings start with something innocent and then grow into something unintended. This happened to me at a reception in Bangladesh.

During one of my many trips to this country, I was invited to a post-conference reception at a private home. It was a lovely place, with plenty of space for the sixty people who attended. I socialized with several of the participants before finding an empty seat on one of the many couches. A small cat jumped on my lap. I petted it for several minutes. Then, without warning, it jumped on the lap of the woman seated next to me. I thought nothing of it. A friend joined me, and we began to chat.

Later that night, Ali, our host, asked, 'Matt, what is it between you and Zareen? She is telling everyone how rude you are.'

Not knowing what he was talking about, I said, 'Zareen who?' He pointed to a woman across the room, the one who had sat next to me on the couch. 'I have no idea what you are talking about. I never spoke to that woman,' I replied.

'She said that you picked up my cat who was seated on your lap and tossed it onto her lap. She called it one of the rudest things she ever saw. She hates cats.'

I felt baffled until I remembered the cat jumping from my lap onto hers. When I went to her to explain the simple misunderstanding, she repeatedly said I was a rude man, then stormed off.

Especially with cats, things happen that can be misunderstood. Most misunderstandings occur because of limited information or false assumptions. How many events in our lives are based on the same thing? How many fights and arguments start from a lack of sufficient information?

Lesson: We must accept that things happen without us knowing all the details. It is important not to get upset with people based on misinformation and uninformed assumptions. Sometimes things just happen. Give others the benefit of the doubt.

The starfish—every life is precious

A recurrent issue I face when making presentations is the fatalistic view that modern slavery problems are too overwhelming and pervasive to tackle. The disparity between 40 million victims and only 100,000 people rescued causes people to question me. They ask, 'With so many victims, it seems impossible to make a difference. Why should we try?' The question arises again and again.

My response is usually the same. I tell them the well-known Starfish Story. This simple parable makes the important point—that every life is precious.

A father and son walk along a beach covered with stranded starfish. Every few feet, the father stoops to pick up a starfish and toss it back into the ocean. At some point, the son looks at the immense stretch of sand, full of dying starfish, and says, 'Father, there is no way you can save all of these starfish. What difference can you make?' The wise father pauses to toss another starfish to safety. In a gentle voice, he responds, 'It made all the difference to that one.'

Every life is important—every life is precious.

The human slavery problem feels so big and so unmanageable that it can easily shut us down emotionally. But this mustn't stop us from doing whatever we can with what we have. To each person rescued, it makes a very big difference. The world gains back a precious grain of humanity with every victim saved from a terrible life.

Lesson: When we work on this or any other cause, victory comes *one life at a time*. Eventually, the numbers will add up to something we never thought possible.

Score from one to ten

Working in a range of developing countries, I sometimes came in contact with diverse management styles. Each style had its own unique and interesting approach. None was necessarily better or worse, merely different.

For example, sometimes government officials would say yes to a proposal of mine when they really meant maybe or no. They often did this out of politeness or a desire to say what they thought I wanted to hear. Since they had no intention to finalize the deal, agreements didn't move forward.

If we don't understand what one of our counterparts feels about something, we can misread the situation. Finding simple ways to gauge a person's feelings can help us understand what is real and what is not.

During a recent marketing project with four Chinese college students, I sensed their discomfort with the direction of the work. Since I wanted to understand their feelings, I asked them to rate how stressed out they felt on a scale from one to ten. Each offered either a nine or a ten. I had my answer.

Realizing that this would interfere with their creativity, we spent the next hour going over various points that caused their anxiety. Through a discussion, we successfully reduced their apprehension. I then went around and asked them a second time to rate their stress levels. It went down to threes and fours.

As my two sons were growing up, I'd use this same technique to gauge how they were feeling about life. But in this case, the question was different. I'd ask them to rate their life from one to ten, with ten being the best. Most times, they'd say nine or ten. If they had a busy period at school, they'd drop it down to eight. This helped me understand where their mindsets stood at any time.

Lesson: We need feedback from those around us. This approach is simple to use and helps to gauge the quality of an interaction or event. I have found people tend to be honest in their answers to this question.

Striving for 'same'

Over the years, we refine our likes and dislikes through trial and error. Through countless repetitions of various behaviors and experiences, we create mental templates that influence future decisions. How many times have we heard someone say, 'I like Chinese food but not Indian food. I like to watch legal dramas but not sitcoms. I like the beach but not the mountains.' At some point in our lives, we create a refined internal list and outline what we think we want and then maintain this list. This is how we maintain 'same'.

Most of us tend to move in the direction of what we think we like and veer away from things we think we don't like. Also, we tend to allow our likes to overshadow what we do not know. An option beyond the list may be considered neutral or undesirable. Throughout life, we refine our options to a sharp point and reject a world of opportunities. In both personal and professional life, such decisions strongly limit our potential. How and why does this process happen?

Experiences define our likes: When something turns out well, we want to repeat the experience. Behaviour psychology is based on this concept: reward and we will repeat; punish and we will stop. But experiences are fickle. Experiences at a Chinese restaurant might be good because of a dozen different factors—the right companions, the right mood, the right food, etc. Repeating the same restaurant choice with different factors would become a different experience. It is a good practice, therefore, to remain open to repeatedly trying and retrying other things before refining our likes.

An experience defines a dislike: If a person goes to a forest for a hike but hates the mosquitoes, heat, or blisters, surely they will conclude that they dislike the forest. Do they dislike the forest, or did they choose the wrong forest at the wrong time of day or year? An inaccurate generalization can result in such events and close us off to a repeat visit and shrink the boundaries of our world.

'Same' is comfortable: Like all habits and routines, 'same' remains comfortable. We know what to expect. As creatures of habit, we like the predictable. As we refine our likes, we also close out alternatives. Think about how you spend your weekends. Do you tend to do the same things, go to the same places, and seek the same kind of entertainment?

For most of us, our days are mired in 'sameness'. What would happen if we had our coffee before taking our shower? What would happen if we got up thirty minutes later or thirty minutes earlier? What would happen if we drove a different way to work, listened to a different radio station, ate a different kind of breakfast, or simply changed some aspect of our daily experience? By doing this, we would be tapping into a rich vein of creativity and changing 'same'.

Remember how it felt to begin a new job? We learned new things and experienced daily and weekly changes. In time, 'new' was replaced with 'same'. The content of the meetings and activities might vary slightly, but then monotony creeps in. In time, few things challenge us. We perform our work on autopilot. When this happens, it's time to make a move. Whenever there is a learning curve, 'same' is held at bay. Learning is a strong antidote to our 'sameness' rut because it adds new insights, experiences, and world views. It alters our life perspective. Such opportunities are good.

Part of the reason why vacations are so special and fun is that we eliminate the sameness of work and home. Experiment for yourself. Try an 'upside-down day', changing everything about it. If you are thrifty, spend money. If you get up early, sleep late. If you eat healthy food, eat something delicious and fatty. This opens you up to 'what if'. What if I changed my life? What if I changed my habits and routines? Could things be better?

Lesson: We are influenced by 'sameness'. Every time we do 'same', we walk away from experimentation—a 'potentiality' is lost.

The element of change—the essence of life

If we watch the course of a river, what is it we see? The superficial answer is a river. But if you look deeper, the answer becomes more complicated. Every second as the water flows, the river changes. Undercurrents shift and move, altering patterns on the surface. Waves appear and disappear at random locations. Each 'instant' for this body of water has unique characteristics that occur and pass away forever. Each moment is unique and happens only once.

Lesson: Each life is like a changing river. Despite our perception that the stream of our lives seems relatively constant, every moment fluidly changes from one to the next.

Embracing the reality of change helps us understand the world around us.

Chapter takeaway

Do any of us really understand much about our existence? Do we ever really stop to put our life into some kind of perspective? To analyze it? To think about it? To learn more about it? The answer to these questions is probably a resounding 'no'. Most of us go through our lives accepting what comes our way, never stopping to realize the complexity, and in some ways the absurdity, of our daily experiences. It is important that we open our minds, to stimulate thought and to motivate ourselves to explore what our life means. Why? Because there are so many fascinating things about life that often go unnoticed. In my opinion, the more we look at the wondrous elements that are continuously unfolding around us, the richer will be our own life experience.

Chapter 14

Today's Abolitionist Movement

With another young man, woman, or child entering into modern slavery every four seconds, we are losing the fight against this crime. I am convinced that the only way to solve this problem is for us to start a second-generation abolitionist movement in which nations and individuals address the crisis. This approach has worked before and can work today. To make this happen, we each must take heroic steps towards freedom for all. We must accept this issue as our own.

Despite what most people think, human slavery is relevant to our lives today. Anything in the world that relates to human rights abuses affects life on Main Street. Free people believe slavery to be a major violation of human dignity. We must actively care about the people with whom we share this world. As beneficiaries of human rights, we must individually accept responsibility for preserving them. When women are forced into prostitution, decent people must address the problem; if they don't, the abuse will just continue. Until now, few of us have accepted this responsibility.

Consumers also contribute to the industries that perpetuate human slavery. With so many human trafficking victims associated with supply chains, we have all purchased goods that are directly or indirectly connected with modern slavery. We must not ignore this reality.

The importance of raising awareness

Over the years, I have made countless presentations on the topic of human slavery for audiences of 5 to 1,500 participants. These audiences meet at schools, corporations, churches, and libraries. In Hong Kong, one year, I presented to nearly 20,000 people. I have learned a few basic lessons about my audiences.

Most people to whom I speak know little about human slavery. Probably fewer than 10 per cent of the people knew even a quarter of the information I shared. If you don't know about a problem, you can't care about it. If you don't care, you won't act. If you don't act, how can we expect our results to improve? Thus, the world's awareness must become a major priority. Everyone must hear the urgent message: slavery is alive and flourishing today.

Once knowledgeable about modern slavery, most people actively care. Almost all are shocked to learn that slavery is so prevalent in this world, with millions suffering in terrible conditions at home and abroad. Here are comments made by those hearing facts about the enslavement of people for the first time:

> *'I am thirty-four years old, and I am finding out about this terrible thing just now. Wow! I don't understand why this isn't front-page news.'*

'I feel terrible that the world doesn't do more about this problem.
Now that I know, I can't turn away. I want to do something.'

'Someone needs to step up and help. I wish I knew what to do.
Give me something to sign up for, and I'll be there.'

While many at this point want to help, you cannot always count on a follow-through. After a presentation, about a dozen people come up and say, 'I was really touched by what you said. What can I do to help?' The people are sincere, but something seems to drain their good intentions. After handing over my business card and agreeing to work with them, I seldom hear from more than one or two again.

There is power in numbers

A few thousand development workers worldwide, despite heroic efforts, cannot solve slavery. It won't go away until world citizens accept this issue as their own and address the problem. Of course, there exists a great divide between wanting to act and taking even small, compassionate steps towards involvement. Finding ways to maintain intense interest in this topic is another major priority.

At the end of most of my presentations, I make this statement: 'If every one of us did at least one thing—just one—this would add up to something great.'

I use the example of the sand dunes I have seen in Cape Cod. These beautiful, massive, natural structures, which seem to rise as high as the pyramids, are made up of millions of tiny pieces of sand. Something great can grow from a massive accumulation of many small things. If each of us offered at least one thing toward the solution, a monumental outcome could result. Therefore, if 10 million people did one thing each, this represents 10 million steps forward.

How can you do your part?

Let's consider a simple list of activities that require little effort. Each such action is a courageous step forward:

Learn and share: Continue to learn about today's slavery and help educate your friends and family. Consult the internet for up-to-date information on this topic. Platforms like Facebook, Twitter, YouTube, LinkedIn, and WhatsApp are all useful. Every person reached potentially adds another soldier to the fight. For our modern-day abolitionist movement to take hold, raising awareness must be a high priority. Helping to get the word out is a heroic activity.

Sponsor an event: Many schools, corporations, faith-based groups, and clubs have stepped up to create awareness. You can invite a speaker for a presentation or a panel discussion. You will find willing speakers knowledgeable on this topic. I sometimes give presentations in private homes. A variety show or musical event can also be organized. Such innovative approaches not only foster awareness but uniquely motivate people and raise money for the cause.

Show a film: There are excellent, compelling films concerning human trafficking/slavery. Most can be watched online for no cost. Consider showing one of these films to your company, school, church, club, or within another community event. The advantage is that people can see exploitation at its worst in the setting where it occurs. This is a highly effective way to educate.

Some films to consider include **Not My Life, Nefarious: Merchant of Souls, The Day My God Died** and **From Darkness to Hope: Transformation of an Ex-Trafficker.**

Become a responsible consumer: Before buying a name-brand item, go online to see if the company has a policy statement about modern slavery. If so, send a quick email to congratulate them. If not, send an email requesting that they post such a statement. These interactions should be positive. A company under attack often pulls back. Encouragement can open up a company and get them to take the steps needed.

Fundraising: Raising money for the cause ranks as necessary heroism. Even small amounts to the right organization can make a tremendous difference in the life of a trafficked person. For example, it costs between $2 and $3 a day—the price of a cup of coffee—to support a deeply traumatized person at a shelter in Cambodia. Funds can be raised through an endurance event, a film showing, a silent auction, and more. Many organizations, both at home and abroad, fight slavery. Before contributing money, contact the organization and ask them to explain how they will use it. Become assured that your money will do what you intend. Check to see if any criticism has been registered against them.

Volunteer: Volunteering is a great way to contribute. You can work at a local NGO office or from home. You might carry out internet searches to collect information for one of the responder groups. To identify an organization, go online and review options. You can find a group that will appreciate your skills and efforts.

Here are some examples of how people have become involved:

- A nine-year-old girl raised $1,500 selling lemonade to help victims of human slavery.
- A college student regularly went to retail stores and politely asked the managers how they ensured the products they sold were slave-free. Eventually, they all offered positive answers. Their main offices took note.
- A housewife wrote letters to newspapers, magazines, and television stations to encourage them to publicize human trafficking and slavery issues, and they did.
- A church ran a songwriting contest titled 'Battle of the Bands' to create awareness among music lovers.
- A mother of three convinced her library to make books available on this subject.
- A college student set up a film festival that reached 5,000 students.
- A father of three got the motels in his city to put the anti-trafficking hotline number in every office.
- A student group sent letters to their state lawmakers, asking them to focus on this issue.
- A fifth-grade class encouraged their local school board to partner with students to include the issue of modern slavery in their curriculum.
- A church group held an all-night prayer session concerning slavery and its victims.

We must use individual talents to fight slavery. Artists can create a human slavery project for public display. Filmmakers can create movies on modern slavery. Writers can write about the issue. Whatever you do, do it in the direction of freedom. Raise your voice if you are a teacher, social worker, doctor, lawyer, or anyone else.

Why do so few people act?

As noted in earlier chapters, many of these suggestions are simple, but too few people follow through. To help find an answer to the basic question, 'Why do so few of us actively care?' I interviewed many people who have attended my talks. Below are some of the more common answers:

It makes me feel bad – Some people can't face the topic of human slavery. It makes many of us feel sad and depressed. People often say to me, 'Reading about this will ruin my day. I don't want to feel sad.' To avoid these feelings, they avoid the topic. I know this because of the reactions people reported about my book on forced prostitution. Most people who started to read *Captive Daughters* wouldn't go past page seventy-nine, where the rape scene unfolds. So here you have someone who is sitting in their living room, on their couch, with the air conditioning on, a cup of coffee in hand, and they can't even face words on a page. Imagine if one of us were on the receiving end of this problem. Shouldn't such a horrific reality spur us to act?

As I have noted repeatedly, I agree that the topic of human slavery is a hard one. It displays the worst life has to offer— rape, torture, abuse, pain, suffering, depression, oppression, despair, betrayal, and more. There is really no way to sugarcoat it. For us to fight this problem, we must understand, feel the pain, and act. We must take action despite our squeamishness. We must learn horrific facts, then get involved. Forty million slaves around the world are crying out, 'Where are you?' We must answer.

To offset this reaction, I often offer a more nuanced approach. I try to balance the horrific situation versus humankind's highest hopes and efforts to save lives.

In Bangladesh, I would see the most beautiful lotus flower growing in a disgusting cesspool. In even the most terrible situations, we can find potential for beauty, love, hope, and positive change. Had I not believed this, I could not have worked among human cesspools in beautiful countries for more than thirty years.

It is so far away – Most believe the problem to be important, but see it as distant, something happening in countries like Nepal, Thailand, or China. Facts about slavery are upsetting but remote. In every presentation, I explain that slavery exists in every nation, but it is hidden. For many, it could be in their own neighborhood.

What difference does it make? – Modern slavery is only one among many important human issues like global warming, terrorism, poverty, war, hunger, and disease. With so many other problems in the world, how can any one person help? It seems hopeless. To a certain extent, we in the counter-trafficking world must take responsibility for this impression. We have failed to convince others that there are many ways to fight this overwhelming human problem as an ordinary person.

Information overload – Most people today are faced with a constant stream of information fed to them through their phones, tablets, TVs, and computers. As a result, important issues like human trafficking and modern slavery might never enter their consciousness.

Me, me, me – Complacency and apathy prevail in some people's lives. Narcissism fosters the belief that life should only be about happiness, prosperity, and fun for me. Nothing else matters. There is little room in this equation for helping others.

Allergy to action – The idea of doing something for others goes against the grain of some people's lives, so action never materializes.

Overcoming human inertia is vital to overcoming modern slavery. The difference between what our world is and what our world can become depends on each person's actions.

Why do we do this work?

In 2009, a man named Simon Sinek delivered one of the most popular TEDx Talks. In it, he offered something truly insightful. He said that people aren't inspired to do business with us because of what we do. They are inspired to do business with us **because of why we do it.**

I am curious to know if he's right. He also described a successful marketing formula. Adjusted for the cause of human trafficking, it might go like this:

> *Within the movement that I'm a part of, challenging the status quo is vitally important. Our efforts often are urgent and*

life-saving. We challenge the status quo by closely collaborating
with local governments to help protect people from human
trafficking, by aiding police in the rescue of slaves, and by
restoring the broken lives that have been horrifically exploited.
What we do is enlarge the world by saving one life at a time.

Here's another way to put it using Simon Sinek's formula:

If you're the kind of person who believes everyone should be free
and you have always dreamed of being the hero who saves the
day, then boy do we have a cause for you! We at the Mekong
Club equip businesses to root slavery out of supply chains. We
educate migrants so that traffickers don't trick them. We arm the
public with knowledge about slavery, one of the most appalling
human rights abuses of our time. We fight so no one is enslaved.

Most people passionately believe that all humankind should be
free. No one should experience violence, abuse, exploitation,
or rape. No one should be forced to work eighteen hours a
day, seven days a week for little or no pay. This happens today
to at least as many people as those who saw the Simon Sinek
video: easily tens of millions of lives.

The impact of modern slavery and business

Slavery impacts every single business in the world. The
majority of men, women, and children are exploited for manual
economic labour in the private sector. They mine, pick, fish,
build, clean, and sew 24/7 under the threat of violence. It is a
global problem on the world stage. The only two countries not
affected by slavery are Greenland and Iceland. Despite global
media attention and the work of NGOs and governments

around the world, the problem grows worse each day. With the COVID-19 pandemic upon us, the needs are greater than ever.

It is now time that businesses enter the battle to free the world of slavery. Legal business has to fight the illegal business of slavery. Change is needed, and the Mekong Club, the organization I run, is the catalyst for this real change. This is a game changer in eradicating slavery. Never before has big business united to connect the best minds in the private sector to develop business ideas that will destroy slavery and equip companies with the tools to fight it.

Though reliable, up-to-date information about human slavery exists in the media, and witnesses offer testimonies to courts and on public platforms, the news receives little notice. If this is because the public is indifferent to human trafficking, I have to ask, Why are we settling for the status quo of forty million slaves? Why don't we work harder to stop this?

Each contribution adds up

Actually, many people are doing something. If you give to a poverty relief programme, sponsor a child, donate to a recovery shelter, support a rescue organization, or do community development work, then you're making a meaningful contribution. Please continue. If you can, increase the time and money you give, because with millions of slaves in the world, there's always scope to do more.

If you run a business and ensure your supply chain is free of slave labour, you're doing one of the most vital jobs possible. Thank you.

If you're in law enforcement, the military, or the medical field, trained to watch for signs that a person might be the victim of human trafficking, you are part of the frontline of detection. Thank you for your service. Please share what you know with others.

Are you a policymaker in a company or governmental agency? How we handle migrant workers and trade agreements has a profound impact on the vulnerability of people to trafficking. Please think carefully about what you do. Seek out experts and weigh the consequences of your policy decisions.

But what about doing more? Maybe we don't do more to stop human trafficking because we don't believe we can make a difference when, in fact, without realizing it, we already are. We must stay encouraged to increase our efforts.

Many people escaped from trafficking because decent people cared enough to donate to a charity that helped the police investigate brothels or labour sites and organize a rescue. Groups like Freeland, International Justice Mission, and Nvader do heroic work that is often risky. Once rescued, survivors are sheltered and nurtured by such organizations as Hagar International, Hope for Justice, and Maiti Nepal. Websites such as Free2Work and Slavery Footprint enable consumers to identify brands with forced labor in their operations. There are so many excellent, competent anti-slavery groups out there, but they cannot operate without your financial support.

The impact of transparency legislation

Recently, laws have been passed to help encourage the private sector to play a more active role in eradicating slavery. In January 2012, the California Transparency in Supply Chains Act went into effect. This applies to all retailers and manufacturers with annual global revenues of more than

$100 million that do business in California. In March 2015, the UK's Modern Slavery Bill was passed into law. This is designed to tackle slavery throughout the UK and consolidate previous offences relating to trafficking and slavery. It includes a new provision on transparency in supply chains, which will require firms doing business in the UK to report on measures taken to ensure any goods produced or services provided by workers are free of slavery and trafficking, and putting legal responsibility on company directors to enforce this. Similar laws have been enacted in France, Australia, and the Netherlands. Similar legislation is also being considered in Canada and Hong Kong.

The status quo

Do you believe in challenging the status quo? The status quo is millions of victims of human trafficking at any given moment. Will you become a hero? Will you be the voice that says, 'I'm going to do something about this? I will not turn my back on people in misery and despair. I will help them out of deplorable situations and stand by them until they stand on their own with dignity. I will help protect others against similar tragedies.'

Help us. You and I are the everyday heroes who hear and answer young victims' cries. It is time we smashed the status quo and changed mindsets.

Thirty years ago, Gita asked me, 'Where were you?' That day, she called us all out and asked why the world didn't help her and other girls in slavery. Throughout the world, there are millions of people in forced prostitution and forced labor who repeatedly ask this same question every day. I am continually reminded of Gita's angry challenge to me and others like me.

After nearly thirty-five years in the field, I am considered an expert. However, to this day and at this moment, I still cannot answer Gita's question or some of the other relevant questions: Why do we, as a world, not care enough to do everything possible to end this systematic rape and slavery? Why is it so hard for this topic to rise to the top of every government's agenda?

This testimonial reflects a scenario that takes place every four seconds as another person becomes a slave. It is worth reflecting on this kind of situation before answering these questions.

I was only fifteen years old when I was sold to the brothel. I was so young. I didn't know anything. I was innocent then. My parents were tricked by a neighbour into thinking I'd be working at a restaurant as a waitress in the city. I wanted to go. I wanted to help my family. I was willing to work. But this is not what followed. After walking through the jungle and crossing the border on a night boat, a van took me to a bad place—a place where girls like me were sold like animals to the owner. When they told me what I was supposed to do with men, I said no, never. I fought back. But that didn't stop them. They abused me and tortured me for days until I had nothing left to give. I no longer had control of my life or my body. I belonged to them. Every night I was with up to ten different men, seven days a week, 365 days a year. For years, this was my life. Now at eighteen, my body is frail from the illnesses. I feel completely empty inside.

People often ask me what happened to Gita. I honestly don't know. I never heard from her again. Tragically, I have to assume she died of HIV/AIDS, along with the hundreds of women and girls I met who were forced to have sex in those terrible brothels. But her question didn't die. It lives on today. If you have read this far, I hope you, too, want to offer an answer to Gita's question. And I also hope you have come to the conclusion that you can take action to help end slavery. As the English abolitionist William Wilberforce said, 'You may choose to look the other way, but you can never say again that you did not know.'

An American woman I met, incredulous at the information this book exposes, said it gave her a vivid flashback to a scene more than fifty years ago. Her seven-year-old son ran into the house after school, red-faced and sobbing so hard she thought something terrible had happened to him. She wrapped her arms around the child and tried to calm him. When he could speak, he cried out, 'Where were you when Hitler killed the Jews? Why didn't you stop him?' She explained to the child that those events happened far away, and she was a child his age and could not have stopped him. 'Where was grandmother then?' he cried. 'Far away from what was happening, and they didn't print stories like that in the newspaper. We didn't have television then; we just didn't know,' she replied.

The memory still pained her because she was helpless to assuage the child's grief, and clearly he did not accept her words as anything more than excuses. That woman asked me, 'If Hitler killed six million people and the world remains revolted by that bestiality, why don't people rise up today when the United Nations says there are more than forty million people worldwide who are now slaves?'

I told her that the estimates are real and growing. She could hardly grasp the fact that North America alone has hundreds of thousands of young people languishing in slavery. The child waiting for a school bus, the teenage runaway, the young woman offered a modelling job in a distant country all vanish with only local attention. Even as the internet helps us track down criminals and rescue a few victims, it also facilitates criminal activity. In most cases, the lure is love or money. Young people want to secure better jobs and too often believe what they read on the screen. Young women in many countries want Western husbands and offer themselves to strangers. The advertisements are convincing, the young people are eager to improve their situations, and hardly anyone can intercept the traps.

If the Holocaust still remains on the world's conscience, why do we not care that six times that number of people, many of them children, have vanished into brief lives of unspeakable cruelty, exploitation, and deadly disease?

Slavery has existed for as long as history has recorded the human race. The only thing new about the issue is the speed and deadliness of its proliferation. While calloused business people make billions of dollars and unsuspecting citizens throughout the world purchase their slave-made products, the numbers of slavery victims now exceeds the population of Canada. Throughout the ages, voices have been raised to greater or lesser effect. Perhaps it's children's voices that will pierce through our excuses, like that of the boy who wanted to know, 'Where were you when Hitler killed the Jews?' or the uncomfortable question from Gita, who demanded of me, 'Where were you? You sit there interviewing people and writing reports. What good is that? I waited and hoped that someone would come help me. Where were you?'

My final appeal

Thousands of years ago, Moses spoke on behalf of the enslaved Israelites and demanded of Egypt's Pharaoh, 'Let my people go!' As America's president, Abraham Lincoln, the Great Emancipator, said before Congress, 'In giving freedom to the slave, we assure freedom to the free—honourable alike in what we give and what we preserve.'

Like Lincoln and those who fought with him, each of us must become an abolitionist. The passion for freedom exists and remains through every generation; it must become even stronger throughout the world at this time. Together, let us answer the question Gita and forty million other men and women, boys and girls are urgently asking us right now: 'Where are you?' We are here, we have heard, and we must act! If each one of us becomes an abolitionist, perhaps one day millions of freed people can shout the unforgettable words of Dr Martin Luther King Jr: 'Free at last, free at last; thank God Almighty, we are free at last.'

Why do I feel this is possible? Because you are already a hero. You have always been a hero. Throughout your life, you have helped, supported and showed kindness to other people. Please stop and think about this. Reflect upon all the good you have already done. Now, own it. Say to yourself, 'I am a hero. I have done good things. I have added my contribution to this world, and I can do so much more.'

Even the fact that you are reading this book on modern slavery and have got this far in the text demonstrates your commitment to learn and grow emotionally and perhaps spiritually. Learning more about this terrible crime against humanity is one of the first steps in the process. Now it is time to act. Consider taking the process one step further.

Over the years, despite efforts from many very committed organizations and individuals, we've had little impact on reducing modern slavery. We need everyone's help to take on this monumental issue. It is time that we all stop thinking about things and **simply act.** It is time that each and every one of us takes a stand. Please consider making a personal promise to help even more by saying the statement below out loud and sticking to it:

> *I have heard about the forty million men, women, and children who are in forced prostitution and forced labor, and want to declare that I consider this to be a terrible crime against humanity. I will do whatever I can to learn more about this important issue and pass this information along to others. I will pass on this message to those in my family, workplace, and community, and commit myself to help in whatever way I can. I will do my part to be there for those in modern slavery who are in great need.*

Now that you have accepted this new responsibility, you might consider changing the way you look at your daily efforts. Accept that each and every day can be filled with heroic acts—big, or small. Look for them, find opportunities to help, take note of them, and have them become a regular part of your life. Feel good, and congratulate yourself. It feels good to do good.

But it shouldn't end there. Educate others about this problem—teach them, inspire them, and reward them. Doing good can be contagious and spread like wildfire. We need to be leaders for both ourselves and for others.

Expand your horizons. Begin thinking beyond your immediate world. Realize that each week you can do one, five, or ten things to make the world a better place.

When my father became old and fearful of falling when he was walking, I suddenly became much more self-conscious when I saw other elderly people walking slowly or with canes. I began to empathize with these people because I had come to understand my father's personal fear. After I was diagnosed with prostate cancer, I would talk about my journey, and many people would tell me their own stories. Before I knew it, I realized how many people were affected by this disease.

If we expose ourselves to the wrongs of our world, we become sensitized to them. Our emotional response compels us to take a stand. Empathy is most often the fuel that drives our good deeds forward. With this in mind, keep reading about this topic. Keep talking about it. Keep advocating for change. As Malala Yousafzai, a Pakistani activist for women's education and the youngest Nobel Prize laureate, once said, 'When the whole world is silent, even one voice becomes powerful.'

We need to constantly remind ourselves that time passes quickly and think about our lives. At least once a week, we should ask ourselves if we are living up to our personal best in our efforts to fight this problem. If not, we can make changes. You have the raw capacity to be heroic with your own unique gifts. Please accept the call to action to get involved and help us end modern slavery. It's that simple.

Annex A

Checklist – Steps to Help Stop Human Trafficking

Learn

Review human trafficking/slavery-related websites online

Watch one or more of the many human trafficking films (e.g., *Not My Life, Nefarious, Human Trafficking, The Day My God Died*)

Attend lectures or panels on the topic within your community

Read one or more of the many books on the topic (e.g., *Good News About Injustice, Disposable People, Priceless*)

Set up a Google Alert on the phrases 'Human Trafficking' or 'Modern Slavery' to get daily or weekly emails with the latest articles or blogs

Memorize the basic information about human trafficking, along with the statistics

Listen to free podcasts (e.g., *Ending Human Trafficking* by Sandra Morgan and Dave Stachowiak)

Take the **Slavery Footprint Survey** and let people know your score

Share

Discuss this issue with your family members, friends, and co-workers

Share the information with your family members, friends, and co-workers through email or social media

Engage your school, church, clubs, or community organizations with information and events

Develop a presentation on the topic and deliver it in a group setting

Organize and sponsor awareness-raising events in your community, such as a presentation from an expert, a film screening, or a variety show

Set up an art exhibition on the topic of human trafficking, including paintings, photography, or sketches

Teach

Teach young people about the techniques used by traffickers to attract victims

Teach young people that traffickers hunt at malls and other places where teenagers congregate, often posing as representatives of modeling agents or other legitimate businesses

Teach young people that traffickers often prey on young people through social media and chat rooms

Report

Report situations that do not seem right to the police, other authorities, or counter-trafficking hotlines

Report cases to the police or other authorities (teachers, counselors, etc.) when a child is with an adult who doesn't appear to be a family member

Report cases to the police or other authorities when a young teenage girl is with a much older 'boyfriend'

Report cases to the police or other authorities when an underage girl is seen selling sex on the street

Report cases to the police or other authorities when a domestic worker is never allowed to leave a home

Encourage

Encourage your local government to review existing laws and procedures on human trafficking/slavery

Encourage your local police to identify and respond to trafficking situations

Encourage your local authorities to employ qualified and well-trained law enforcement officials, judicial officers, prosecutors, investigators, detectives, border guards, and anti-trafficking police

Encourage your local school to provide formal training on the topic in classroom settings

Encourage your federal government to make this a priority issue

Encourage your local newspaper or television station to cover stories about human trafficking

Encourage local businesses and corporations to get involved in helping to address the problem

Consume responsibly

Go online and see if the companies you buy from have codes of conduct or policies to address human trafficking (knowthechain.org)

Congratulate the companies that do have codes of conduct or policies, and politely encourage those that do not to take action

Support those companies that appear to be taking the issue seriously through your purchases

Give

Donate to a local or international human trafficking/slavery program—no amount is too small

Sponsor a fundraising event to help raise money for a worthy organization

Volunteer

Donate your time or expertise to a local organization fighting this problem

Donate your time or expertise to an organization in another part of the country or internationally using the internet

Use your talents and Be Creative

If you're a writer, write a blog; if you're a painter, paint a picture; if you do sports, use this platform to raise awareness and funds; if you sing, write a song; if you like movies, create a short film and post it

Commit

Commit to doing up to five of these actions per year—or even more if you can

Commit to taking part in the emerging global abolitionist movement

Publicly pledge your support to this important cause

Acknowledgments

I would like to begin by acknowledging the support provided by my lovely wife, Sylvia, who has believed in me and my work from the beginning. I would also like to acknowledge the unwavering support provided by my father and mother, my two sons, and the rest of my family. You have always been there for me during my many ups and downs. For this, I am most grateful. I love you all.

As for those who supported me throughout my career, there are too many to list. You know who you are. I would like to take this opportunity to express my deepest gratitude for your advice, guidance, kindness, and love. I would also like to thank those of you who challenged me with rebukes and criticisms, and for the drama you introduced into my work. These life experiences have also influenced me, and I have learned many lessons from them.

Finally, I would like to thank Brian Mansur, Charlotte Hale, Karen Cooper, and Matthew Keeler, who helped edit and refine the manuscript.